'An excellent and engaging introduction to the climate crisis. This book shows us
how we can all make sustainable choices and change our world for the better.
Definitely worth a read for any young planet protectors!'
AMY BALL
Primary Education Officer, WWF-UK

'Every home and school needs this book.'
NICOLA DAVIES
Children's Book Author

'A delightful take on the most serious subject of our times. A must read for youngsters and all those
concerned about the future of our youngsters.'
CHRISTIANA FIGUERES
Former Executive Secretary of the UN Framework Convention on Climate Change

'*Climate Action* is a perfect book for us to use through our Roots & Shoots programme,
which works with many schools throughout the UK. Lots of trees will be planted!'
DR JANE GOODALL, DBE
Founder of the Jane Goodall Institute
& UN Messenger of Peace

'This beautiful, accessible and inspiring book should be available for every child.'
CAROLINE LUCAS
Green Party MP

'This is an excellent guide that is full of colour and charm. A great way to teach
children about climate change and inspire a new generation of climate leaders.'
SEÁN MALLON
Climate Change Specialist, WWF-UK

'There's so much in this book. Facts, statistics, illustrations, and alternatives,
but most importantly it is packed with hope. This is the book the world really needs.'
BENJAMIN ZEPHANIAH
Poet, Author and Musician

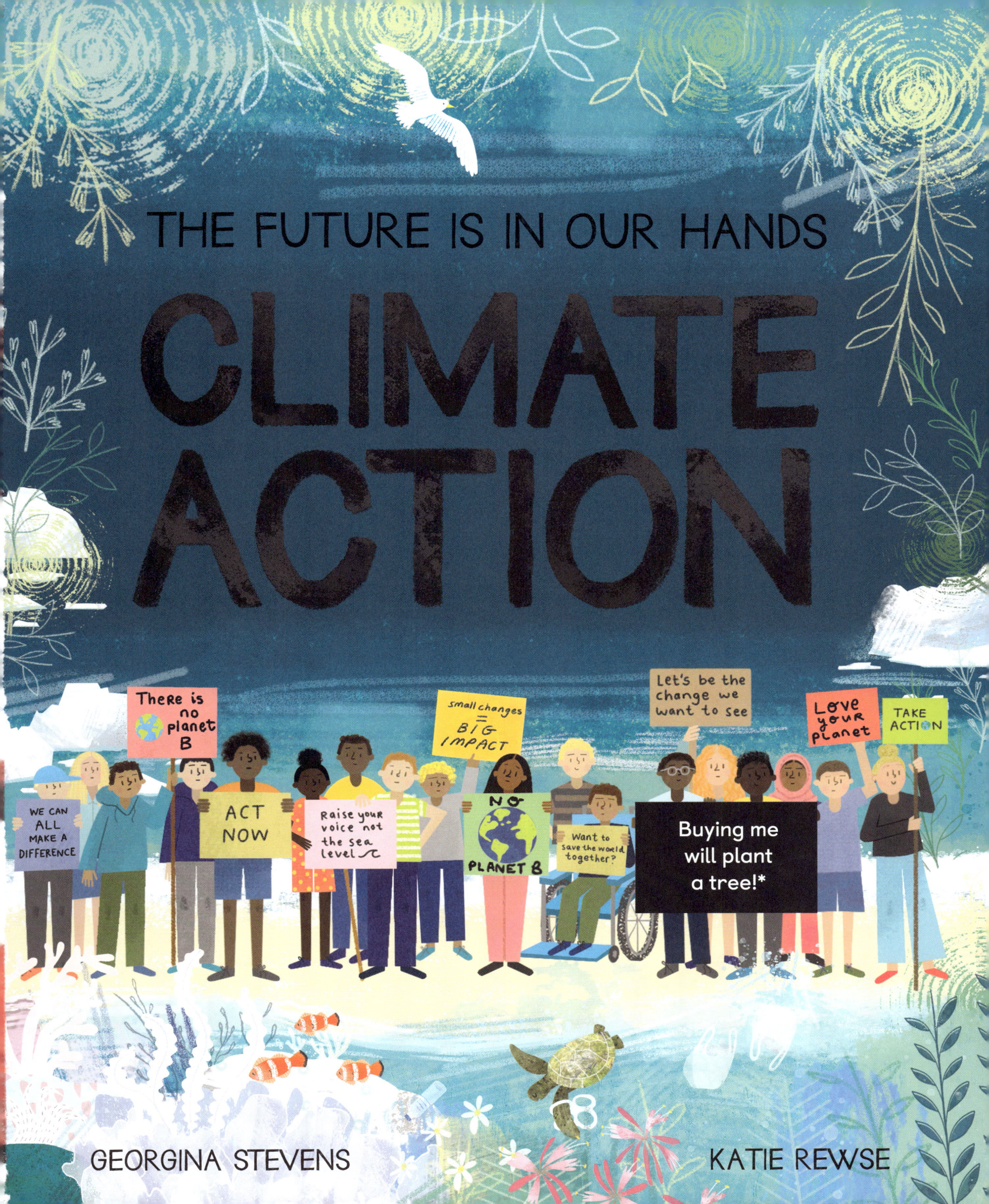

For Rafael, and all you world changers out there; let's all be the change we want to see.

Georgina Stevens

To Mum, Dad and Dean for your endless support and inspiration.

Katie Rewse

The world is an ever-changing place and the people within it are capable of incredible things; discoveries are made, records are broken, new facts are found and history recovered. We will be happy to revise and update information in future editions.

*We will be planting a tree with the charity TreeSisters for every copy of this edition sold in the UK. TreeSisters fund ethical, community-led reforestation projects in the tropics.

The Forest Stewardship Council® (FSC®) is an international, non-governmental organisation dedicated to promoting responsible management of the world's forests. FSC operates a system of forest certification and product labelling that allows consumers to identify wood and wood-based products from well-managed forests and other controlled sources.

For more information about the FSC, please visit their website at www.fsc.org

LITTLE TIGER
LONDON

360 DEGREES
An imprint of the Little Tiger Group
1 Coda Studios, 189 Munster Road, London SW6 6AW
Imported into the EEA by Penguin Random House Ireland,
Morrison Chambers, 32 Nassau Street, Dublin D02 YH68
www.littletiger.co.uk • First published in Great Britain 2021
Text by Georgina Stevens • Text copyright © Georgina Stevens 2021
Illustrations copyright © Katie Rewse 2021
A CIP catalogue record for this book is available from the British Library
All rights reserved • Printed in China
ISBN: 978-1-83891-161-4 • CPB/5000/2078/1221
2 4 6 8 10 9 7 5 3

CONTENTS

4 Foreword
5 Introduction

CAUSES
7 Climate Change
8 Greenhouse Gases
10 Energy
12 Agriculture
14 Deforestation
16 Transport
18 Buildings
20 Mining

EFFECT
22 Climate in Crisis
24 Rising Sea Levels
26 Flooding
28 Tropical Storms
30 Coral Reefs
32 Droughts
33 Heatwaves
34 Biodiversity Loss
36 Wildfires
38 A Hotter World

OUR PART
40 Our Carbon Footprint
42 Our Food
44 Our Clothes
46 Our Homes
48 Our Stuff
50 Our Travel

INSPIRATION
52 Groundbreakers
54 How to Get Active
55 Climate Changer
56 Green Futures
58 What Next?

60 Glossary
64 About the Creators

FOREWORD

Ever since I planted my first tree at the age of seven, I have envisioned a world where we will live in harmony with nature – a world where we will put people and our planet before profits. This kind of world will only be possible if we start viewing the climate crisis as an emergency. Mother nature has repeatedly warned us that we need to start treating her better, but we have continued to ignore her. Everyone should be held accountable for the consequences of failing to act. It's not fair to leave young people and future generations to clean up a mess that they did not create.

Growing up in the most forested region in Kenya – Nyeri County, made me love nature and connect to it at a young age. It broke my heart when I saw or read about how the world's forests were being destroyed, how the lakes, rivers and oceans were becoming a soup of poison flowing with plastic waste, and how the climate crisis was negatively impacting people around the world. Everything was happening so fast and I was greatly worried about the future of our planet. Therefore, I decided to become a voice of change.

We who see the urgency must continue to rise up, act, speak up, and demand urgent climate action. We are the only hope and we must keep fighting to secure a livable world now and a safe future.

Elizabeth Wathuti

Elizabeth Wathuti is an environmentalist and climate activist. She founded the Green Generation Initiative, which engages young people with environmentalism and has planted over 30,000 trees in Kenya. She is Head of Campaigns and Daima Coalition Coordinator at the Wangari Maathai Foundation. Elizabeth has won many accolades, including UN Young Champion of the Earth and Africa Green Person of the Year Award 2019. She was also named one of the 100 Most Influential Young Africans by the Africa Youth Awards.
www.greengenerationinitiative.org

INTRODUCTION

This book is about changing the world for the better.
It's about how we all have the power to make a real difference.
And it's also about the many incredible young people, just like you, who are already taking action at a time when change is most needed.

Earth is home to many millions of different species of animals, plants and organisms, as well as some amazing habitats. We are very lucky to live on such an incredible planet. But our world is changing fast, and we are in the midst of a climate and biodiversity crisis.

This book will help you to understand what climate change means for us and for the future of planet Earth. We will look at the causes and how the natural world is being affected, and we will explore the ways in which our lifestyles can impact the planet.

Most importantly, this book will show you some of the positive and effective actions that are being taken to combat climate change and loss of biodiversity, from tree-planting to campaigning. And you will meet some amazing young changemakers from all over the world who have taken matters into their own hands. There's even a handy glossary at the back in case you come across any words you don't know.

The ideas in this book might inspire you to take action, learn more or come up with ideas of your own. Even small changes can have a big impact because they might encourage others around you to make changes too. For every copy of this edition sold in the UK we will be planting a tree with TreeSisters, who fund community-led reforestation projects in the tropics. I am also using my royalties to share copies of *Climate Action* with brilliant charities that are helping young people to fall in love with nature and learn about taking action, including WWF-UK, Jane Goodall's Roots & Shoots and Eco-Schools England. Thank you for taking the time to read this book.

Georgina Stevens

CAUSES

THE MAIN REASONS FOR THE CLIMATE
CRISIS AND A GLIMPSE INTO THE FUTURE

CLIMATE CHANGE

Climate change describes a shift in Earth's weather patterns over a long period of time. These include more frequent and powerful extreme weather events, rising temperatures and changes to rainfall sequences. Our climate is transforming faster now than it has for the last 1,000 years.

THE GREENHOUSE EFFECT

Energy from the Sun passes easily through our atmosphere and heats the surface of the Earth, where our land and seas absorb it. In return, Earth emits heat; some of it passes through the atmosphere and out into space, and some is absorbed by a layer of greenhouse gases that sit above the atmosphere. The greenhouse gases send part of that energy back down again, warming the surface of the Earth and the lower part of the atmosphere.

GLOBAL WARMING

Global warming is the long-term rise in temperatures across the world. The average surface temperature on Earth is now 1.1°C (1.9°F) higher than it was between 1850 and 1900, before large-scale fossil fuel burning began.

LAYER OF GREENHOUSE GASES

ATMOSPHERE

WHY IS THE CLIMATE CHANGING?

Most greenhouse gases, such as CO_2 and methane, occur naturally in the atmosphere. They are able to trap heat – without them, Earth would be a chilly –18°C (0.4°F), rather than our average temperature of 15°C (59°F). Unfortunately, many of our activities over the last 100 years have increased the levels of all of these gases. This means that they are trapping more heat than ever before, changing the climate and making the planet a lot hotter.

'Carbon dioxide' and 'CO_2' mean the same thing. We will use both terms interchangeably throughout this book.

CAUSES

Natural causes of global warming do exist – the Sun's strength varies over time and Earth's orbit shifts, which changes the amount of sunlight it receives. However, the main cause is the increase in greenhouse gases being leaked into the atmosphere, mainly through the burning of fossil fuels.

FOSSIL FUELS

Oil, coal and gas are fossil fuels. They were formed over millions of years from decomposing organisms. When we burn fossil fuels to make energy, greenhouse gases are released into the air.

GREENHOUSE GASES

In 2019, we pumped over 43 billion tonnes (47 billion short tons) of carbon dioxide alone into our atmosphere. The major sources of greenhouse gases are shown below. Are you surprised by any of them? Thinking about your own life, is there something you could change which would help to reduce your own contribution to our rising emissions?

ELECTRICITY AND HEAT PRODUCTION — 30.4%
The biggest cause of rising greenhouse gases is our burning of coal, natural gas and oil to produce electricity and heat for buildings.

ENERGY USE IN MANUFACTURING, CONSTRUCTION AND OTHER INDUSTRIES — 21%
We burn a lot of fossil fuels to make and build things. We also produce plenty of greenhouse gases directly when we make materials such as cement, ammonia and metals.

AGRICULTURE, FORESTRY AND LAND USE — 18.3%
When trees are cut down and burnt to make way for agriculture, they release the CO_2 that they have absorbed during their lifetime. Livestock farming produces a lot of methane when animals burp and fart!

TRANSPORT — 15.9%
Vehicles are responsible for a lot of fossil fuel burning. There are now more than one billion combustion engine cars on the roads.

FUGITIVE EMISSIONS — 5.8%
Gas leaks from oil and gas pipes and coal mines produce a significant amount of global greenhouse gases.

COOK STOVES — 5.5%
3 billion people cook using wood, kerosene, biomass or coal, which produces significant levels of dangerous indoor pollution and greenhouse gases.

WASTE — 3.1%

Methane is released from landfill sites from rotting rubbish, and waste water treatment causes other greenhouse gases to be produced.

WHAT CAN WE DO?
Talk about climate change, global warming and greenhouse gases with your friends and family, and ask your school to cover it in more detail.

HUMAN-MADE GREENHOUSE GASES IN OUR ATMOSPHERE

CARBON DIOXIDE 76%

Carbon dioxide is the least potent of the greenhouse gases, but we have produced far too much of it from burning fossil fuels, and it remains in the atmosphere for thousands of years.

POSITIVE FEEDBACK
Water vapour is a naturally occurring and potent greenhouse gas. As human-made greenhouse gases increase and warm our planet, water vapour also increases, pushing temperatures up even further.

Fluorinated gases (F-gases) are the most potent greenhouse gases. They can stay in the atmosphere for up to a thousand years. They are found in fridges, air conditioning units and aerosols.

METHANE 16%

Methane is able to trap much more of the Sun's energy than CO_2. Luckily, it only sticks around for about ten years, but there are large stores of it in the ice and the seabed, which could heat things up really quickly if released. Two thirds of methane comes from decaying waste in landfill, burping and farting livestock, and leaks from fossil fuel mining.

F-GASES 2%

NITROUS OXIDE 6%

Nitrous oxide is a powerful greenhouse gas because it stays in the atmosphere for about 100 years and damages the ozone layer. About 40% of nitrous oxide in the atmosphere is the result of human activity, mainly agriculture.

HISTORY REPEATS ITSELF
The amount of carbon dioxide in the atmosphere is measured in parts per million (ppm). In 2019, concentrations of CO_2 were around 415ppm and are predicted to rise to 427ppm by 2025. The last time Earth experienced a similar level of CO_2 was 15 million years ago; humans didn't exist, temperatures were 2-3°C (3.6-5.4°F) hotter and the sea level was up to 20 metres (65ft) higher than it is now.

WARMING STRIPES
The warming stripes, devised by British climate scientist Ed Hawkins, show annual temperatures from 1850 to 2019, with darker reds representing the warmest years. They make it clear that it has got a lot warmer over the last 15 years!

DID YOU KNOW?
One third of all methane is naturally produced by peatland, wetlands and farting termites! Termites produce tiny amounts of methane but it adds up to some 20 million tonnes (22 million short tons) each year because there are so many of them!

1850   2019

ENERGY

Just 150 years ago, we burnt wood for warmth and to cook and mainly used animals to move things around. Today, we burn a lot of fossil fuels to power our lives, and energy use is now the biggest source of greenhouse gases. The good news is that our incredible planet provides us with many types of renewable energy from natural sources. And some of them are cheaper than fossil fuels, too. So next time you switch on a light, think about where your energy has come from and use it wisely!

WIND ENERGY

More than a third of the world's wind power comes from China and this is growing fast! Wind turbines harness kinetic (motion) energy and the generator turns it into electricity. The tallest wind turbine is twice the height of the Statue of Liberty!

Wind turbines inspired by hurricane-resilient palm trees are being developed. Their blades flex in the wind like leaves and they can survive extreme weather.

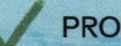 **PRO**

It's thought that wind could provide as much as 30% of the world's energy needs.

 **CON**

The wind doesn't always blow (but ways of storing excess energy are getting more efficient).

OCEAN ENERGY

Tidal power is the only renewable source derived from the Moon. It uses the rise and fall of tides to convert kinetic energy into electricity.

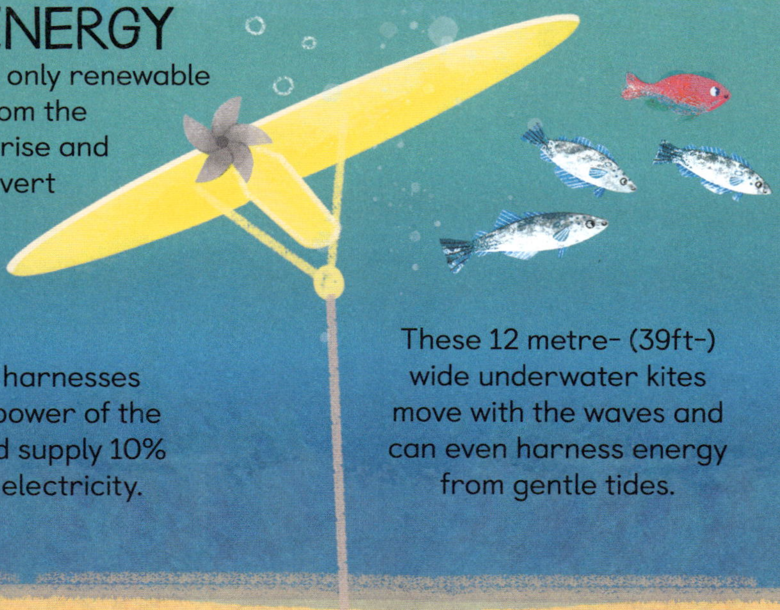

Wave energy harnesses the enormous power of the waves and could supply 10% of the world's electricity.

These 12 metre- (39ft-) wide underwater kites move with the waves and can even harness energy from gentle tides.

WHAT CAN WE DO?

Renewable energy tariffs provide electricity from suppliers who use energy from renewable sources. Why not ask your school or parents if they have a renewable energy tariff? It will reduce their carbon footprint and shouldn't cost any more money. In fact, it might be cheaper! It will certainly reduce the environmental cost to the planet...

 PRO

Constant and predictable source of energy.

 CON

Machinery is expensive and can damage marine ecosystems.

SOLAR ENERGY

The Sun could provide a year's worth of energy in just one hour if we could harness it all! Solar panels absorb the Sun's energy and convert it into electricity. Solar mirrors work differently. They reflect sun rays into one area and convert the heat into energy.

✓ **PRO**
It is a very cheap form of power and solar panels can be recycled.

✗ **CON**
Solar panels are made from mined silicon, which produces hazardous chemicals. Only a small number are recycled today.

Lots of new islands are popping up in lakes and seas around the world... They are sun-seeking solar islands covered in panels that move to face the light, just like sunflowers!

HYDROELECTRIC ENERGY

Hydropower is one of the oldest energy sources on the planet. It was used in ancient Greece to grind grain and has been harnessed ever since. Flowing water spins a turbine, which generates power.

✓ **PRO**
Reliable in areas with plenty of rainfall.

✗ **CON**
Local habitats are affected by the large flood zones and rotting vegetation can produce lots of methane.

BIOMASS ENERGY

We are unlikely to run out of this one, as any waste product can be converted into biomass energy, including animal poo!

✓ **PRO**
Algae can be used to make different types of fuels. They grow quickly and are high in energy.

✗ **CON**
Not all sources of biomass are sustainable. Some cause deforestation or release pollutants.

GREEN HYDROGEN

There's more hydrogen than anything else on our planet, but most of it is stuck in water. However, once the oxygen is removed from water using renewable energy, it can be used to power all sorts of machines, including cars!

✓ **PRO**
Twice as efficient as petrol when used in a car.

✗ **CON**
It takes a lot of energy to remove hydrogen from water, so it is currently expensive.

GEOTHERMAL ENERGY

The largest geothermal spring is in New Zealand – it is the size of six football pitches! Geothermal energy comes from heat deep inside the Earth. It can be obtained directly from hot spring water or through the capture of steam (which moves turbines that power generators).

✓ **PRO**
Available at all times, in many areas around the world.

✗ **CON**
Pumping high-speed water into rock to access geothermal energy can cause earthquakes.

AGRICULTURE

Over 11,500 years ago, humans began planting grains and later on, domesticating animals. This was the beginning of agriculture and today it takes up about one third of all land on Earth. There are still many farmers around the world who rent or own small farms, but in wealthier countries large scale industrialised agriculture has taken over. Although this can enable the production of more food, it also generates significantly higher greenhouse gas emissions, and it can have a very negative impact on the local environment and our own health. But we need to grow food for everyone somehow. How would you grow yours?

FOOD, AT WHAT COST?

SOIL

The world is losing 30 football pitches of soil every minute! This is caused by activities such as the over-use of pesticides and fertilisers, which can reduce the micro-organisms in soil.

BIODIVERSITY LOSS

Biodiversity is lost when land is cleared or monocultures are grown. Many animals, particularly pollinators, are severely affected by the use of pesticides and other chemicals.

WATER

Agriculture uses 70% of Earth's precious freshwater, and the release of fertilisers, pesticides and other chemicals or waste can pollute groundwater, rivers, streams and oceans.

GREENHOUSE GASES

Deforestation and land clearance for crops and livestock cause the release of CO_2; fertilisers release nitrous oxide; and cows and sheep burp and fart a lot of methane.

CARETAKERS OF OUR LAND

Farming doesn't have to be damaging! **Regenerative farming** aims to breathe life back into the land through conservation and rehabilitation. Farmers work in harmony with nature, encouraging biodiversity and carbon dioxide storage, rejuvenating the soil and increasing the land's resilience to climate change. All without ploughing!

Organic and biodynamic farming techniques oppose the use of chemical pesticides. Both use compost and manure instead of man-made fertilisers. Some biodynamic farmers also use the phases of the Moon in deciding when to plant crops.

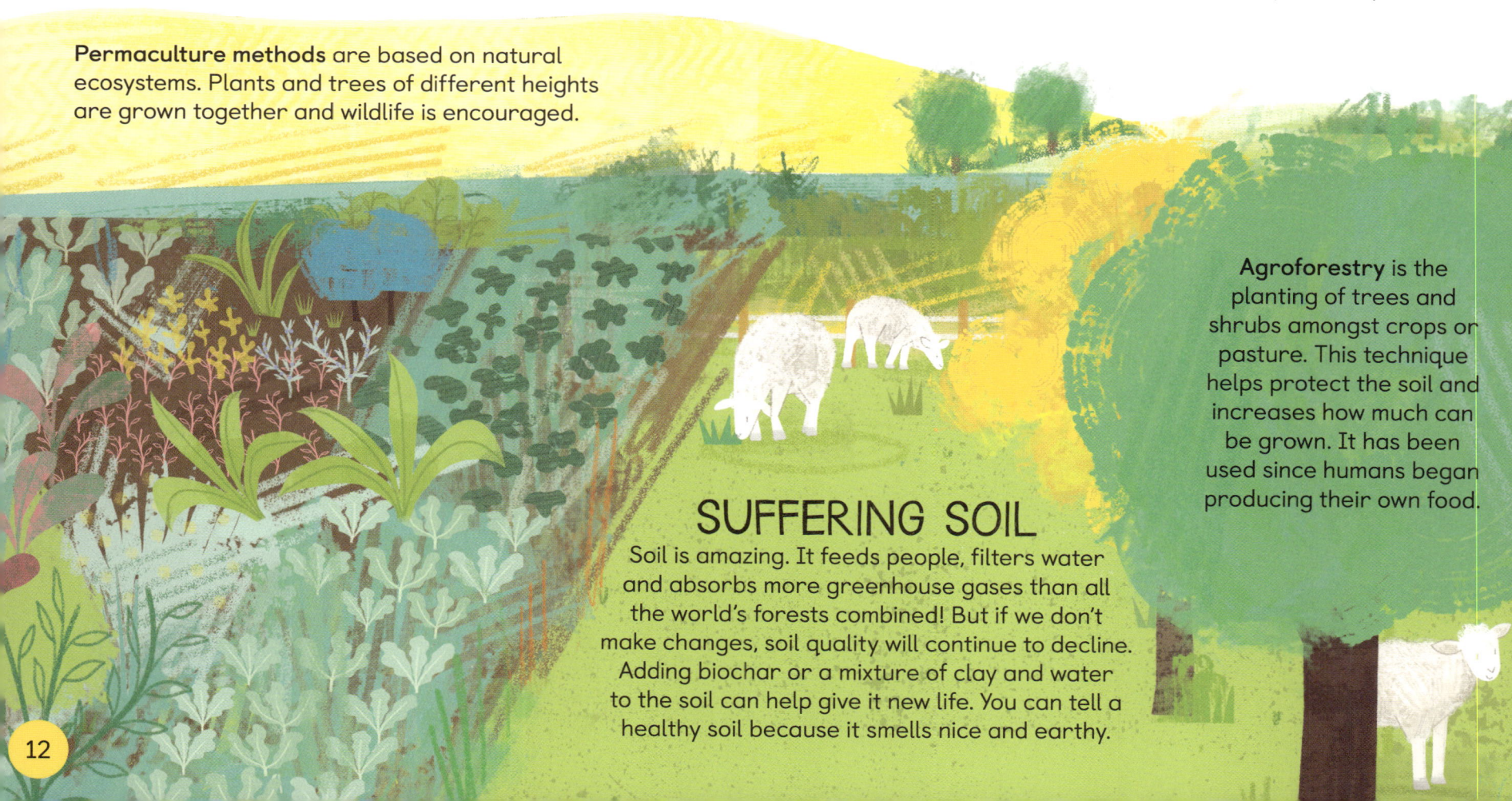

Permaculture methods are based on natural ecosystems. Plants and trees of different heights are grown together and wildlife is encouraged.

Agroforestry is the planting of trees and shrubs amongst crops or pasture. This technique helps protect the soil and increases how much can be grown. It has been used since humans began producing their own food.

SUFFERING SOIL

Soil is amazing. It feeds people, filters water and absorbs more greenhouse gases than all the world's forests combined! But if we don't make changes, soil quality will continue to decline. Adding biochar or a mixture of clay and water to the soil can help give it new life. You can tell a healthy soil because it smells nice and earthy.

changemaker

Mikaila Ulmer
Texas, USA

When Mikaila Ulmer was four, she learnt that bees were at risk due to the pesticides used on farms. Using a family recipe, she made lemonade with local honey and sold it to raise money for charities who are trying to save the honeybees. Mikaila now sells her lemonade in a large chain store.

WHAT CAN WE DO?

You don't need to be a farmer to save the soil! Soil in allotments and gardens is generally healthier, and produces up to 11 times more than some farms! So why not grow your own food? If you don't have a garden, use a window box, apply for an allotment or garden share with someone.

Worms cannot thrive in soil with microplastics, so you can help them by picking up litter.

FARM-FREE FOOD

Scientists are experimenting with turning bacteria from soil into many different food types, from flour and oil to eggs, meat and fish, in a process called precision fermentation. This could change the way we produce our food forever and could help save the environment, just in the nick of time.

DID YOU KNOW?

There are more organisms in one teaspoon of healthy soil than there are people on Earth. And it takes 100 years to create just 1mm (0.03in) of topsoil.

VERTICAL FARMING

Some pioneers are planting upwards to save space! Plants are grown in water or mist instead of soil, and stacked in layers. LED lights mimic sunlight, and pesticides are not needed.

Farmers are experimenting with seaweed, adding it to the feed of their livestock to reduce the methane they burp!

DEFORESTATION

Forests are amazing. They are home to incredible animals and plants and are our best defence in the fight against the climate crisis. But every year, over ten billion trees are cut down and many are dying. Climate change weakens trees, dries out their soil and strengthens the insects that feed on them. At this rate, rainforests will only survive for another 100 years. If they go, we will lose 80% of all plant and animal species. Let's all speak up for the trees!

MAIN CAUSES

AGRICULTURE
Forests are cleared to raise livestock or to plant soya, oil palms and other crops.

LOGGING
Trees are cut down (often illegally) so that their wood can be used for fuel or other products.

MINING
Mining for fossil fuels, precious gems and metals causes deforestation and pollutes local areas.

WILDFIRES
Wildfires burn down huge areas of forest, and climate change is increasing their frequency and impact.

DEFORESTATION HOTSPOTS

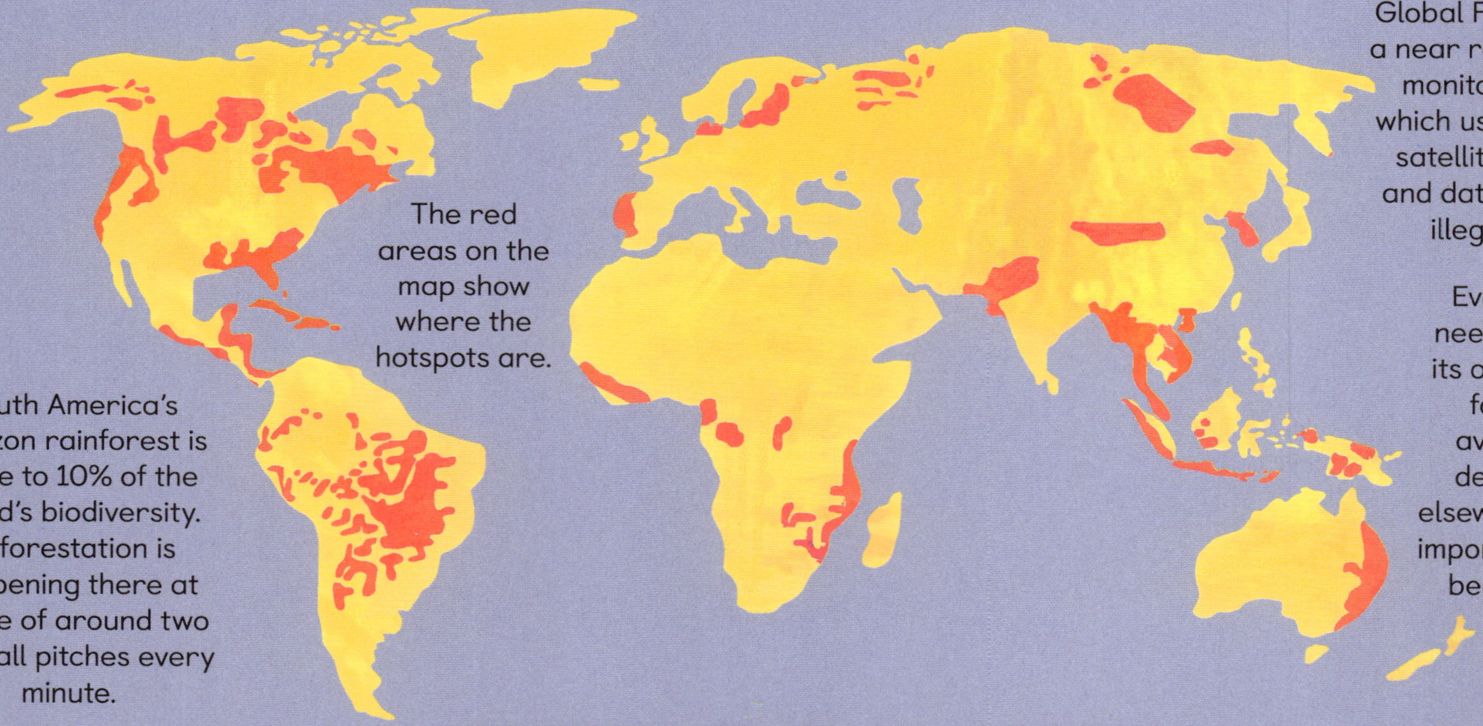

The red areas on the map show where the hotspots are.

South America's Amazon rainforest is home to 10% of the world's biodiversity. Deforestation is happening there at a rate of around two football pitches every minute.

Global Forest Watch is a near real-time forest monitoring system, which uses algorithms, satellite technology and data to help fight illegal logging.

Every country needs to protect its oldest original forests and avoid causing deforestation elsewhere through imports of palm oil, beef and soya.

TERRIFIC TREE PLANTERS

Eight Latin American countries are reforesting an area the size of Uruguay.

The United Nations plans to restore trees to an area bigger than India.

Africa's Great Green Wall will stretch across the width of the continent. It will be the largest living structure on the planet when it is finished – three times the size of the Great Barrier Reef!

Pakistanis planted a billion trees in 2017. Their target is ten billion!

In celebration of Earth Day 2020, 7.8 billion trees are being planted; one for every person on the planet.

changemaker

Felix Finkbeiner
Munich, Germany

Felix founded a global movement, **Plant-for-the-Planet**, when he was just nine. The movement has planted over 13.6 billion saplings and engaged 78,000 youths as Climate Justice Ambassadors.

"Stop talking, start planting."

WHAT CAN WE DO?

Look out for the FSC logo on wooden products. It shows that they were sustainably sourced, including this book!

Use the online search engine that uses its profits to plant trees – **ecosia.org**

Plant trees with a local tree planting scheme or adopt one near where you live and water it during the summer.

GREEN WALLS

Long bands of trees, known as green walls, are springing up all over the world. They reduce CO_2 and air pollution, and animals like them too! China is planting one along the edge of the Gobi Desert. Over 66 billion trees have been planted so far!

SEED MACHINES

Drones are being used to spray seeds, which could make planting trees quicker and cheaper in the future. But we still need people to manage the forests to ensure they thrive.

↙ BISON

ELK ↗

BROWN BEARS ↙

GREY WOLVES ↙

LET NATURE BE

Often, the best thing to do is leave an area alone. But sometimes nature needs a little help... Rewilding – the practice of leaving the land to return to its natural state, as well as reintroducing native plants and animals – has had some wild results! Grey wolves were reintroduced to Yellowstone National Park in 1995. They help to keep deer populations in check, which in turn helps the trees to thrive and support many other species.

WILD BOAR ↘

LYNX ↙

15

TRANSPORT

Travelling by road, railway, sea or air, and moving goods around (freight) produces a lot of pollution, as most of our travel still relies on the burning of fossil fuels. Emissions from cars and planes are polluting the air we breathe, and the oceans are being contaminated by the huge number of ships transporting goods and people. Surely it's time for change?

DID YOU KNOW?
When you're in a car, the polluted air from traffic jams is worse for you to breathe in than it is for pedestrians walking along that same busy road.

GOOD NEWS ON THE GROUND
Road transport is the biggest and fastest-growing area of transport emissions. But change is happening...

Hyperloops, which use sealed tubes and magnetised tracks to move people and freight around very quickly, are in development. Maybe you will ride the hyperloop one day – it might be faster than the old school bus...

Several countries are bringing in bans on cars that run on fossil fuels, and many cities are limiting the use of cars to improve air quality.

There are more electric and hydrogen vehicles around the world now, including the odd electric ice-cream van! We will start to see solar-powered vehicles soon too.

It takes more energy to make an electric car than a car with an engine, but when driven, electric cars produce fewer emissions. Especially if they are charged up using green energy!

Some countries are trialling Electric Road Systems, where vehicles are recharged as they drive along.

UP IN THE AIR

Flying contributes up to 5% of global carbon dioxide emissions. More and more people want to fly and explore new places, so if we are to achieve a zero-carbon world soon, we need some changes!

Electric, hybrid and hydrogen planes will soon be flying passengers on short flights, greatly reducing emissions and noise pollution.

Solar panels have been trialled on planes and one has made a round-the-world flight! Research is also being carried out on solar panels that could convert CO_2 from seawater into methanol jet fuel!

Unfortunately, electric vehicles require batteries, which impact the environment. The metals inside them come from mines and if not disposed of properly will leach chemicals into the soil.

ALL AT SEA

Shipping uses a lot of toxic fuels, which cause air and water pollution, but 90% of goods are carried to us by sea! So next time you buy a new phone or jumper, think about the journey they have made to get to you.

A battery-powered barge capable of carrying 280 shipping containers is being developed. It will run for 34 hours between charges.

When ships reduce their speed by 10%, they produce up to 30% less CO_2. That's a big difference to the planet for slowing down a little bit!

Ships are trying out different ways to reduce their emissions, including using large kites that pull them along! Some cruise liners are trialling the replacement of fossil fuels with biofuels made from leftover fish and organic waste. The crew love their new zero-carbon fuel but say the boat is a bit stinky!

changemaker

Lathika Chandra Mouli, Singapore

Lathika has developed a system to help electric car owners buy solar-powered charging stations. They can offer this service to other electric car owners, and any excess energy can be sold to the power grid. Lathika was made a UN Young Champion of the Earth for her work!

WHAT CAN WE DO?

Can you cycle or walk to school? If not, try out a bicycle bus! They have electric motors for those steep hills and can carry up to 11 children.

Ask for locally made or pre-loved gifts for your birthday.

Find out where your food is from. Try to avoid air-freighted food, but if you love tropical fruit, buy Fairtrade to ensure local workers are paid fairly.

BUILDINGS

Buildings and their construction have a big impact on the environment. They produce greenhouse gases, chemicals, air pollution and waste, and often destroy ecosystems. Concrete buildings can worsen the effects of climate change by speeding up flooding, absorbing heat from the Sun and trapping air pollution.

CONCRETE

Look outside in any town or city and you will see a lot of concrete! It is the second most-used substance after water. In 2019, 4.1 billion tonnes (4.5 billion short tons) of cement was produced. Half of it was made in China.

CEMENT

Cement is needed to make concrete. It requires heat at a temperature of 1,450°C (2,642°F) – almost as hot as a meteor! One tonne of cement produces more than a tonne of CO_2.

Globally, the building industry is responsible for using:

12% of all drinkable water

35% of all natural resources

36% of global energy

INNOVATIONS

Some builders reduce their use of concrete simply by adding vegetable particles or bamboo fibres to it. And more concrete is being recycled now, too.

Researchers are trying to create 'living concrete' out of bacteria. It absorbs CO_2 and can even mend itself! There is also a type of cement being developed that can absorb air pollution, using sunlight to break it down.

The world produces enough steel to build an Eiffel Tower every three minutes! A lot of coal is used to make steel, so it has a very large carbon footprint. But clever people are trialling green hydrogen to produce steel, which makes it much cleaner!

Natural building materials store carbon rather than emit it. This building is made of bamboo, which is fast-growing, strong and flexible.

LIVING ROOFS

Green roofs can be created from plants grown on the top of buildings. They tackle air pollution and reduce flooding by absorbing rain water. They are also good insulators, meaning buildings need less heating and cooling!

Wooden buildings are coming back into fashion. Many are being made from mass timber – wood compressed into fire-resistant beams, columns and panels.

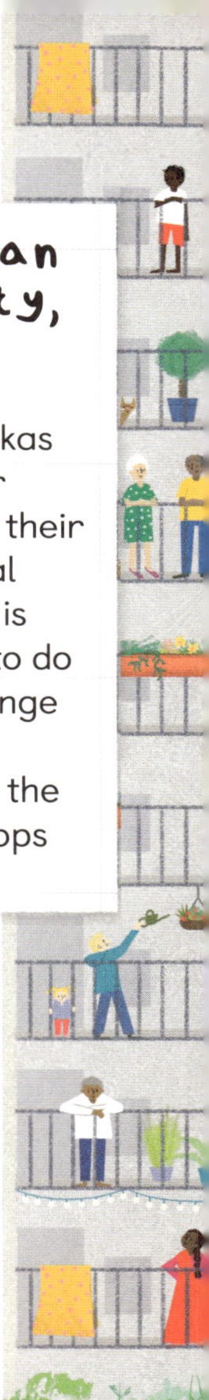

changemaker

Kaisanan Ahuan Nantou County, Taiwan
Kaisanan is part of the indigenous group of Taokas people. He is fighting for their rights and sharing their knowledge in the Central Taiwan Plains. Kaisanan is asking the government to do more about climate change and stop the damaging construction projects in the Plains. He holds workshops about the climate crisis.

WHAT CAN WE DO?

If your street is full of concrete, you could ask your local council to plant more trees. Perhaps your school has room for extra greenery or a vegetable garden? Could you offer to help?

Concrete patios increase temperatures and water run off, so if you have a garden let it breathe and grow wild!

URBAN FOREST

China is planning to build the world's first forest city. Liuzhou Forest City will have one million plants and 40,000 trees, mostly on the outside of buildings. The city will absorb 10,000 tonnes (11,000 short tons) of carbon dioxide each year.

MINING

Mining is the removal of minerals and metals from the Earth. It causes pollution, loss of biodiversity and soil and it can displace people. Illegal mines are common and particularly damaging to the environment.

DEEP-SEA MINING

Companies now want to mine the ocean floor, which could release a lot of stored carbon and lead to significant loss of biodiversity. But it could also help us find solutions for storing renewable energy. What would you do if it was your decision? Perhaps we need to mine the information further...

WHAT DO WE MINE AND WHY?

METALS
Copper and iron are used for building. Gold and silver are precious metals.

FOSSIL FUELS
Coal, oil shale, petroleum and gas are burnt to create energy.

GEMSTONES
Diamonds, rubies, sapphires, emeralds and other precious stones are used for jewellery.

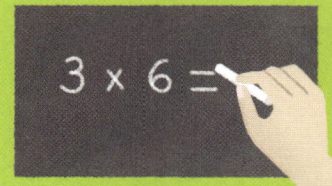

MATERIALS
Minerals are used to make fertilisers, as well as beauty and health products. Chalk and limestone are used for building.

NEGATIVE IMPACTS

Air pollution can occur when minerals are exposed and toxic materials are released. It can be very dangerous for animals and humans.

URBAN MINING

Instead of digging up precious ecosystems, we could mine urban areas! There is so much metal and concrete from disused buildings and electronic waste that could be recycled. Do you have any old laptops or phones you could donate to a charity to recycle for you?

Ground pollution is caused by the release of poisonous waste from mines, which contaminates the ground and makes the soil unproductive.

Water pollution is caused by the release of toxic substances into local waterways, such as poisonous mercury, which is used to extract gold.

WHAT CAN WE DO?

Most batteries use mined elements so avoid them if you can. If you need batteries, opt for reusable ones and recycle dead batteries to stop them polluting landfill sites.

DID YOU KNOW?

Around 40 million tonnes (44 million short tons) of methane leaked from coal mines in 2018. These accidental leaks are worse for the environment than a year's worth of emissions from the aviation and shipping industries put together.

EFFECT
THE WAYS IN WHICH OUR WORLD IS CHANGING

WILDFIRES	HEAVY RAINFALL	DROUGHTS	FLOODING	EXTREME STORMS	HEATWAVES

WHAT CAN WE DO?

Read about how climate change is affecting other countries to get a better view of the issue.

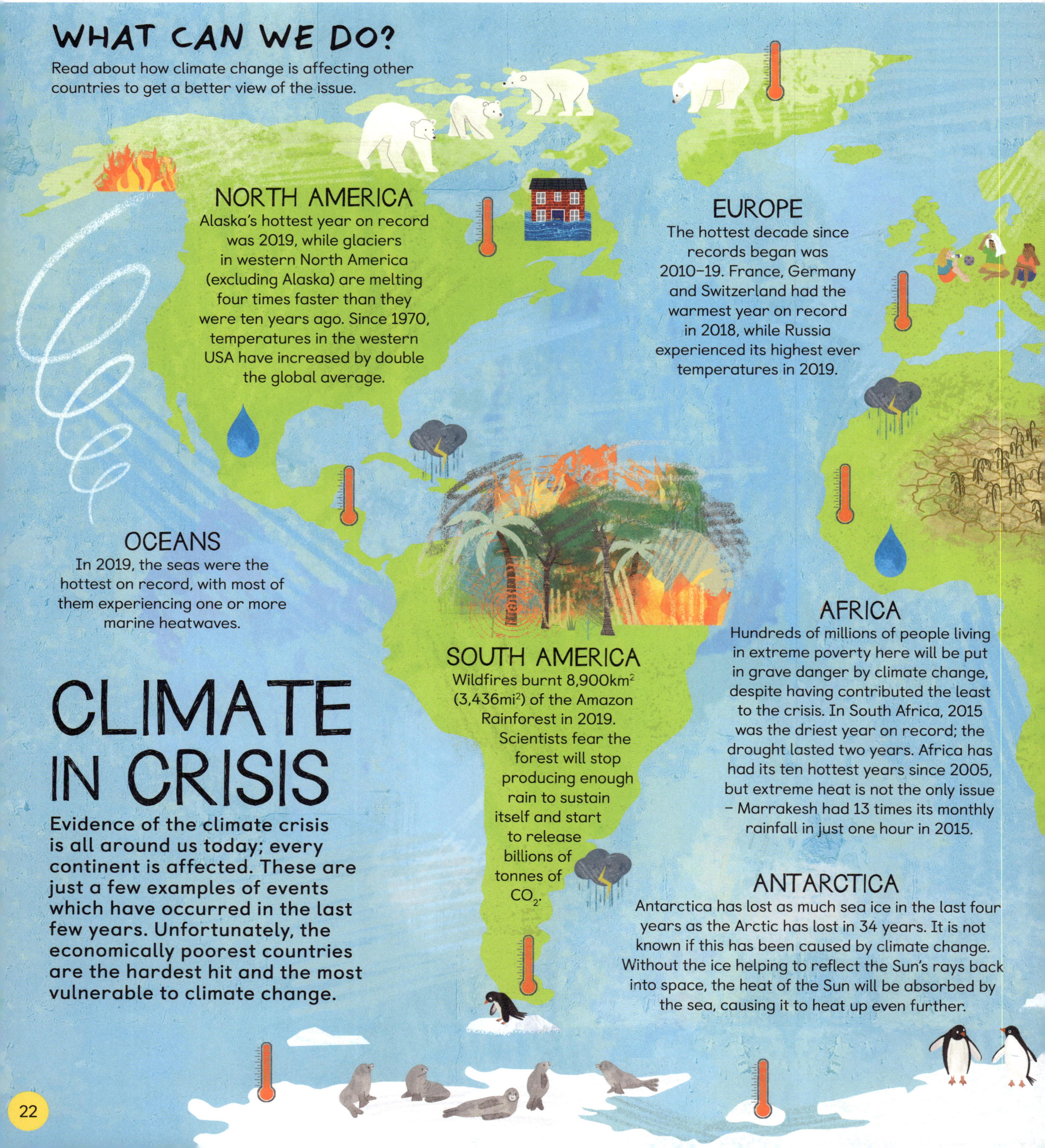

NORTH AMERICA
Alaska's hottest year on record was 2019, while glaciers in western North America (excluding Alaska) are melting four times faster than they were ten years ago. Since 1970, temperatures in the western USA have increased by double the global average.

EUROPE
The hottest decade since records began was 2010–19. France, Germany and Switzerland had the warmest year on record in 2018, while Russia experienced its highest ever temperatures in 2019.

OCEANS
In 2019, the seas were the hottest on record, with most of them experiencing one or more marine heatwaves.

SOUTH AMERICA
Wildfires burnt 8,900km^2 (3,436mi^2) of the Amazon Rainforest in 2019. Scientists fear the forest will stop producing enough rain to sustain itself and start to release billions of tonnes of CO_2.

AFRICA
Hundreds of millions of people living in extreme poverty here will be put in grave danger by climate change, despite having contributed the least to the crisis. In South Africa, 2015 was the driest year on record; the drought lasted two years. Africa has had its ten hottest years since 2005, but extreme heat is not the only issue – Marrakesh had 13 times its monthly rainfall in just one hour in 2015.

ANTARCTICA
Antarctica has lost as much sea ice in the last four years as the Arctic has lost in 34 years. It is not known if this has been caused by climate change. Without the ice helping to reflect the Sun's rays back into space, the heat of the Sun will be absorbed by the sea, causing it to heat up even further.

CLIMATE IN CRISIS

Evidence of the climate crisis is all around us today; every continent is affected. These are just a few examples of events which have occurred in the last few years. Unfortunately, the economically poorest countries are the hardest hit and the most vulnerable to climate change.

22

GLOBAL
24 million people were displaced from their homes due to natural hazards in 2016, most of them linked to disasters made worse by climate change.

ARCTIC
The Arctic is warming at least two and a half times faster than the global average rate. This is making soils drier, ice melt faster and causing more wildfires. Rapid ice melt is affecting the ability of indigenous people to hunt and to access resources they need. It also means polar bears are able to hunt for far fewer days each year, impacting their numbers and ability to have babies.

MIDDLE EAST
In 2019, Lebanon suffered terrible wildfires, made worse by a heatwave and strong winds.

Continuing droughts in Syria have been the worst in 900 years, forcing millions of people to move elsewhere.

Droughts and extreme heat have left millions of people in Africa without enough food.

EAST ASIA
Each year, there are about 40 severe storms in the Western Pacific. In 2018 this led to hundreds of thousands of people being left homeless in China and the Philippines.

SOUTH ASIA
In 2018, Kerala in India experienced the worst flooding since 1924 due to unusually high rainfall during the monsoon season. Around a million people were evacuated; many lost their homes. In the last ten years, South Asia has had its hottest years since records began. On average there have been 35 cyclones each year in the Indian Ocean.

AUSTRALIA
Australia has experienced its ten warmest years on record since 2005, with 2019 the hottest and driest. Wildfires swept across the country and one billion animals were killed. New coral growth on the Great Barrier Reef fell by 89% after mass coral bleaching in 2016 and 2017.

RISING SEA LEVELS

The ice caps are currently melting three times faster than they were five years ago. The melted ice adds more water to the oceans while increasing temperatures cause sea water to expand. This explains why sea levels may rise by up to two metres (6.5ft) by 2100, unless we significantly slow or stop our production of greenhouse gases. This rise would leave many major cities (particularly in Asia), at risk of flooding.

SUN
REFLECTED SUNLIGHT
ABSORBED SUNLIGHT

MELTING AWAY

The polar ice caps have been working as a natural cooling system for tens of thousands of years because they reflect some of the Sun's rays back into space. This is called the albedo effect. As they melt, not only are they less able to reflect heat back, but they also release stored greenhouse gases. This further contributes to warming temperatures and more melting ice. It is a very worrying positive feedback loop.

DID YOU KNOW?

Antarctica is actually a desert! The definition of a desert is somewhere with rainfall of just 25cm (9.8in) per year or less.

ON THE RISE

Sea levels are rising at a rate of about 3mm (0.1in) per year. This is partly due to the melting ice caps but also to do with warmer oceans – when water gets warmer it expands. Seas are now about 0.5°C (0.9°F) warmer than they used to be.

changemaker

Nathalie Hoang
Papeete, Tahiti

Nathalie tried to meet Tahiti's Minister for the Environment to raise concerns about rising sea levels but was told she was too young. Ignoring this, she organised the 200-strong Tahiti climate march.

"Rising sea levels are displacing people from low-lying atolls to overcrowded upper islands."

WHAT CAN WE DO?

Do you have a bank account? If you do, why not make sure that your bank is not investing in fossil fuel projects? Write to them or check on this site, which can also give you information about renewable energy tariffs: www.earthdayswitch.org

LAND LOSS

If no action is taken, rising sea levels will mean people have to leave low-lying coastal areas. 37 countries have already lost land. St Kitts and Nevis in the Caribbean has lost more than a quarter of its land area since 1961.

Governments must work together to protect the fragile polar ecosystems from activities such as fishing and drilling, to try to prevent further melt of the ice caps.

RADICAL IDEAS

Some scientists are concerned that the reduction of fossil fuel emissions will not be enough to halt rising sea levels. Some extreme projects have been suggested...

One idea is to spray trillions of tons of snow over west Antarctica to halt the ice sheet's collapse. This would replace the lost ice, push the sheet back down and stabilise it.

Another suggestion is to build a wall to block the flow of warm water near a glacier in west Greenland. This would help to prevent further melting, but the construction would be difficult and potentially dangerous.

Interesting as these ideas are, they are very expensive, energy intensive and so far unproven. The best thing we can do is try to cut out any fossil fuels we use in our everyday lives.

FLOATING CITIES

Many coastal cities may become submerged eventually. One solution is to build cities that can float with rising sea levels. The world's first floating nation is being built off the coast of Tahiti. Perhaps the Minister for the Environment was listening to Nathalie after all!

FLOODING

The climate crisis is causing more flooding. Warmer air can hold extra moisture, leading to more intense periods of rain. Add rising sea levels and more storms and you can see why over 2.3 billion people have been affected by flooding in the last 20 years. Floods can damage crops, homes and livelihoods and can also lead to the loss of many lives. So how can we protect ourselves?

NATURAL FLOOD DEFENCES

WETLANDS

Wetlands are found all over the world in different forms, including swamps, floodplains and mangroves. They are among the most biodiverse places on Earth and are permanently or seasonally flooded – about 6.8 million litres (1.5 million gallons) of flood water can be stored in 4,050m² (1 acre) of wetland. They are also the most at risk from human development, so we need to protect them!

DAMS

Animals can help too! Beavers build dams on rivers so that they can live in safety from predators. Dams filter the water, improving its quality, reducing the speed at which water rushes down a valley and creating natural wetlands.

WATERSIDE FORESTS

These trees grow next to bodies of water. Their leaves slow the impact of rain and the roots help to keep soil in place. Soil can absorb a lot of water, so together, trees and soil provide vital flood defences.

CORAL REEFS

Reefs reduce the impact of floods and storms by slowing the power of storm waves. It is thought that they currently protect around 200 million people.

SEAGRASSES

The erosion of coastlines is slowed down by seagrasses, which trap sediment in their roots. They hold up to 10% of the ocean's carbon but only take up 0.1% of the sea floor.

26

MAN-MADE FLOOD DEFENCES

There are many ways in which we try to defend ourselves against flooding and storms – building sea walls, dredging sediment from waterways, temporary flood barriers and making dams. But many man-made defences are built from – you guessed it – concrete, and they sometimes make flooding worse. Dredging (the removal of natural material from waterways) can speed up the flow of a flood, causing more damage to the surrounding area and wildlife. The best man-made defences are those that mimic nature...

RAIN GARDENS

China is covering roofs and walls with plants to create wetlands and adding lots of greenery to streets in Nanhui to slow down flood water. This has earned it the name 'Sponge City'! China is aiming for sponge status across more of its cities.

OYSTER REEFS

Artificial reefs made of oysters create natural sea walls and slow down storm surges. Oysters are filter feeders, so they also improve water quality and support biodiversity.

WATER MEADOWS

Allowing farmland or wasteland sites to flood and turn into floodplains or wetlands is a very simple and effective way to reduce further flood damage.

SAND DUNES

Dunes provide good natural flood defences, but many need help to avoid the erosion caused by wind and waves. Grasses can be planted on them, or in some areas artificial dunes are built using natural materials, including unwanted Christmas trees!

WHAT CAN WE DO?

Be careful not to trample or damage wetland areas when you are walking in them. Keep to paths where possible.

Find out what your local natural flood defences are and help support them. It might involve planting beach grass or old Christmas trees on sand dunes or protecting local wetlands or coral reefs.

changemaker

Ridhima Pandey
Uttarakhand, India

Ridhima was only six when she saw floods ravage the land. She set up a petition to sue the Indian government for not acting on climate change. It was dismissed but she has escalated it to India's Supreme Court. Ridhima regularly speaks in schools.

"I want to save our future."

TROPICAL STORMS

Tropical storms all feature strong winds, thunder, lightning and heavy rain, often causing flooding and mudslides. Most tropical storms happen around the equator, as they get energy from warm waters. With rising ocean temperatures, stronger storms are increasing, happening over bigger areas and becoming more dangerous.

STORM TRACKING
There are several specialist tropical storm forecasting centres around the world, such as the National Hurricane Centre in Miami, Florida, which use satellite images, weather instruments and computer-based prediction modelling to detect and track tropical storms. When tropical storms are predicted, warnings are issued.

DID YOU KNOW?
Tropical storms move in great towers of wind that can be more than 18km (11mi) high! This makes the world's tallest building (Dubai's Burj Khalifa) look rather small...

BURJ KHALIFA

EL NIÑO
The El Niño-Southern Oscillation (ENSO) is a naturally occurring, periodic change in winds and sea temperature. It can seriously disrupt normal weather patterns and cause extreme flooding and droughts all over the world. The climate crisis is likely to intensify the impact of the ENSO on our weather systems.

METEOROLOGY
The most dangerous thing about storms is their unpredictability – how strong they might be or when they will suddenly intensify. You could consider a career in meteorology and help improve storm predictions.

SUPERSTORMS
Large-scale tropical storms are called hurricanes, cyclones or typhoons, depending on where in the world they occur. To qualify, storms must have wind speeds of at least 119 kilometres per hour (74mph) and they always form over the sea.

HURRICANE PATRICIA
This tropical storm is the most intense ever recorded. Wind speeds of 346 kilometres per hour (215mph) battered western Mexico in 2015.

WHAT'S IN A NAME?
Tropical storms are often given names. They go in alphabetical order, alternating between male and female names. If a storm is particularly deadly, its name is removed from the list. Is there a storm with your name? What can you find out about it?

WHAT CAN WE DO?

Watch weather programmes and follow storm patterns around the world. Think about how they could affect where you live.

Learn to swim or support someone who lives in an area prone to storms and flooding. It could be life-saving.

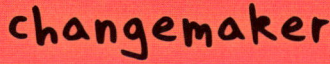

changemaker

**Kawika Ke Koa Pegram
Hawaii, USA**

Kawika was 17 when Hurricane Walaka hit Hawaii and sank an entire island in 2018. Kawika knew he needed to act, so has been climate striking ever since in Honolulu and taking his message to schools in Oahu.

CLASSIFY THE STORM

These categories describe the severity of different storms. There are now more category 4 or 5 storms than ever before. Rising sea levels are also making storms more dangerous as they increase flooding. There is no such thing as a category 6 hurricane or tropical storm (yet).

1
119–153kmph
(74–95mph)

Large tree branches will snap. Extensive damage to power lines and poles.

2
154–177kmph
(96–110mph)

Small tree trunks may snap. Damage to roofs. Near total power loss expected.

3
178–208kmph
(111–129mph)

Many trees snapped and uprooted. Electricity and water may be unavailable for weeks.

4
209–251kmph
(130–156mph)

Roofs blown off and damage to walls. Area uninhabitable from weeks to months.

5
252kmph
(157mph) or higher

Total destruction of homes and buildings. Massive evacuation may be required to keep people safe.

CORAL REEFS

Coral reefs come in all shapes, colours and sizes. They are made up of thousands of tiny marine animals called polyps. Coral reefs occupy a tiny percentage of the ocean's total area, but they support a quarter of all underwater species! They are found in oceans around more than 100 countries, mostly in warm, tropical waters. Reefs can reduce the impact of storm waves by 97% when they are healthy. If global temperatures rise by just 1°C (1.8°F), it is likely that we will lose 99% of tropical reefs.

DID YOU KNOW?
Recently, a coral reef was found in Italy! It is the first reef of its kind found in the Mediterranean. It is a special kind of ecosystem that thrives despite low levels of light. Researchers were very excited and hope that there may be others.

GREAT BARRIER REEF
This underwater ecosystem in Australia is the biggest coral reef on Earth – in fact it is the largest living structure in the world (until Africa's Great Green Wall is finished)! It is composed of more than 2,900 individual reefs and 900 islands, and it stretches over 2,300km (1,400mi). That's almost the length of the entire East Coast of the USA!

DID YOU KNOW?
Every year, eight million tonnes (8.8 million short tons) of plastic ends up in our oceans. That's the equivalent of one rubbish truck every minute.

CORAL BLEACHING
Higher water temperatures place stress on corals, causing them to spit out the algae that they depend upon for energy. This turns the corals white. If temperatures fall, corals can recover, but they will die if temperatures stay high. Around three quarters of warm-water reefs are severely bleached.

UNDER THREAT

Pollution, plastic, sewage, fertiliser, oil – all of these can affect healthy growth and reproduction of coral. When reefs are covered in plastic they succumb more easily to diseases.

Invasive species, such as lionfish, are also an issue. They can reproduce very quickly, and have huge appetites, so can unbalance a coral ecosystem rapidly.

Overfishing of predators and other species, such as parrotfish, which regulate the algae on the corals, can damage the reef ecosystem.

REEF RESCUE

Fragments of wild corals are collected and grown on tree-like structures. Some nurseries are trying to develop heat-resistant corals that can survive rising temperatures.

Fish are attracted to coral reefs that sound full of life, so scientists have been tempting fish back to degraded reefs by playing 'healthy reef sounds' in an effort to repopulate and support them.

One idea which could help heat-stressed corals, is to pipe cool water over them, using energy from ocean waves.

changemaker

Adeline Suwana
Jakarta, Indonesia

When Adeline was 12, her village was flooded. In response, she formed a community of young people called Sahabat Alam (Friends of Nature), which has more than 1,700 members in Indonesia. They support students to plant coral reefs and mangroves, protect turtles, and run beach and reef clean-ups.

WHAT CAN WE DO?

 Never touch or stand on the coral if you are snorkelling or swimming over it.

 Don't buy coral souvenirs when you are on holiday.

 Do a beach clean and geotag the litter on the Litterati app. It shows companies which of their products end up in the seas.

 Use reef-friendly sun cream that doesn't contain nasty chemicals.

31

DROUGHTS

A drought is a prolonged shortage of water from lack of rain or surface water. Almost a quarter of the global population lives in extremely water-stressed countries. Climate change is causing more regular and longer lasting droughts. Severe droughts can reduce the amount farmers are able to grow, destroy farmland and animals, and endanger lives.

FEEDBACK LOOP

Global warming is causing soil to dry out more quickly. This means plants can lose their water supply. If this continues for a long period of time, the plants may die.

When rainfall does come, the drier soils are less able to absorb water, increasing the likelihood of flooding, and washing away the soil.

With fewer plants, rainfall can be reduced because less water evaporates into the air.

FIRE HAZARD

Droughts and heatwaves can increase the likelihood of wildfires and disrupt energy sources.

RAIN MAKER

When air passes over forested land, it produces twice as much rain as air passing over sparse vegetation. Loss of tree cover can decrease rainfall thousands of miles away.

AQUIFERS

These underground stores are formed from water that has trickled down through dirt, sediment and rocks over thousands of years. Companies drill for this water, but with very little regulation from governments. This means that some aquifers are becoming extremely low, leaving certain communities more vulnerable to drought.

DID YOU KNOW?

Some farmers now use drought-resistant crops which can grow with less water.

HEATWAVES

Heatwaves are periods of unusually hot weather in an area, when compared to normal temperatures. Climate change is making them more frequent and severe. If carbon emissions are not curbed, scientists have predicted that searing temperatures will endanger the lives of at least 4% of the world's population by 2100.

Heatwaves are happening all over the world, not just in warm countries. In 2019, multiple heatwaves happened in Australasia, Europe, Asia, Africa and North America. Russia's heatwave in 2010 killed at least 10,000 people.

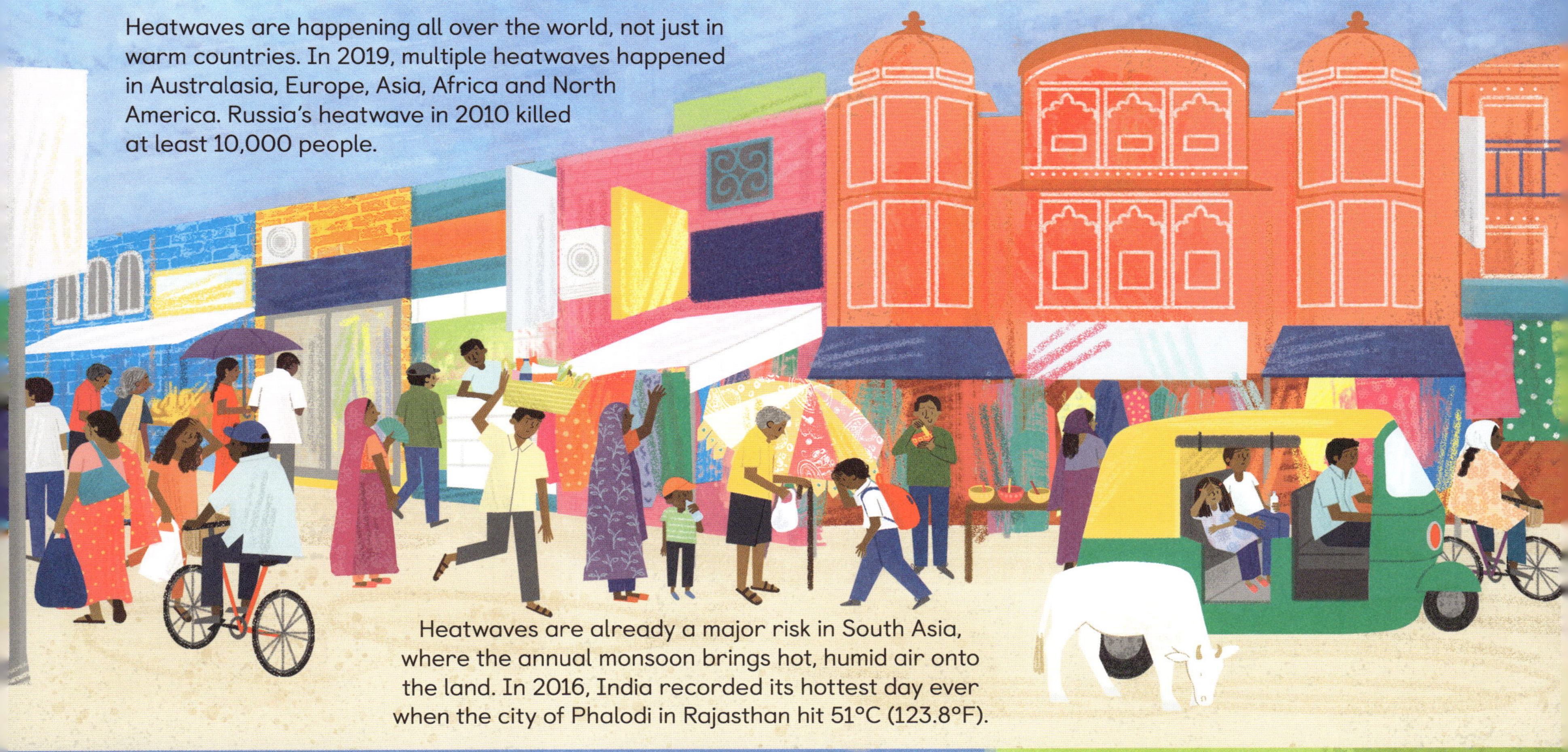

Heatwaves are already a major risk in South Asia, where the annual monsoon brings hot, humid air onto the land. In 2016, India recorded its hottest day ever when the city of Phalodi in Rajasthan hit 51°C (123.8°F).

MARINE HEATWAVES

These occur when the surface of the sea gets very hot. These heatwaves are happening more frequently and for longer because of climate change. In 2016, the Great Barrier Reef was hit by a marine heatwave that killed 30% of the coral.

SOW THE SEEDS

Cities with fewer trees will be hardest hit by heatwaves, as trees provide cooling moisture and shade. Another good reason why we should get planting!

changemaker

Leah Namugerwa
Kampala, Uganda

When Leah learnt about widespread hunger in Uganda, caused by prolonged droughts, she began campaigning to get the government to act, and to get the media to report more fully on the issues. She celebrated her 15th birthday by planting 200 trees.

"I am too young to vote but I'm not too young to make a positive difference."

WHAT CAN WE DO?

Stay hydrated and carry a reusable bottle with you instead of buying water, as the water industry is depleting underground water sources.

Use a water butt to collect rainwater in your garden if you have one, and use it to water your plants or lawn instead of using precious tap water.

33

BIODIVERSITY LOSS

Biodiversity is the rich variation of life on Earth. Around 1.7 million species of animals, plants and fungi have been recorded, but there could be up to 100 million! However, scientists warn that we are entering into an age of mass extinction – we may lose one million species in the next few decades. This is a biodiversity crisis.

MASS EXTINCTION

Earth has seen five large losses of biodiversity in the past caused by natural phenomena such as massive volcanic eruptions, deep ice ages and asteroid impacts. Scientists believe a sixth mass extinction has now begun and this time, humans are the cause. The extinction rate of species is about a thousand times higher than before we were around and animal populations have fallen by about 60% since 1970.

DESTRUCTION OF BIODIVERSITY

We need to address these issues to slow the devastation of the natural world.

Climate change is forcing species to move to cooler areas, making them more vulnerable.

Invasive species which can destroy native species and ecosystems.

Pollution from industries such as mining and agriculture.

Exploitation of resources, including over-fishing, mining, poaching and the exotic pet trade.

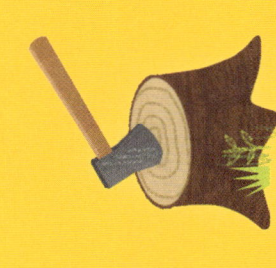

Habitat loss caused by agriculture, deforestation, industry and development.

THE WEB OF LIFE

All living things in an ecosystem are connected, and they all need energy. Plants use energy from the Sun to make their food and grow; they are the only living organism that can do this. Animals get energy from eating plants or other creatures, so the energy moves along the food chain. Every plant and creature, no matter how great or small, is essential in keeping the ecosystem stable, but our activities are putting them all under threat.

The Sun provides energy for plants to make food via photosynthesis.

Fungi and bacteria decompose non-living matter, returning nutrients to the soil to feed plants.

Trees and plants are called producers in the food web – they provide food for the primary consumers.

Bees eat pollen and nectar from flowers, and they help plants reproduce by spreading pollen. They pollinate a third of our food but are at high risk of extinction.

Worms improve soil drainage and oxygenation. They make soil more fertile by breaking down organic matter.

Birds of prey have no natural predators. They help to control the population of smaller animals, so they in turn do not eat too many of the plants at the bottom of the chain (primary producers).

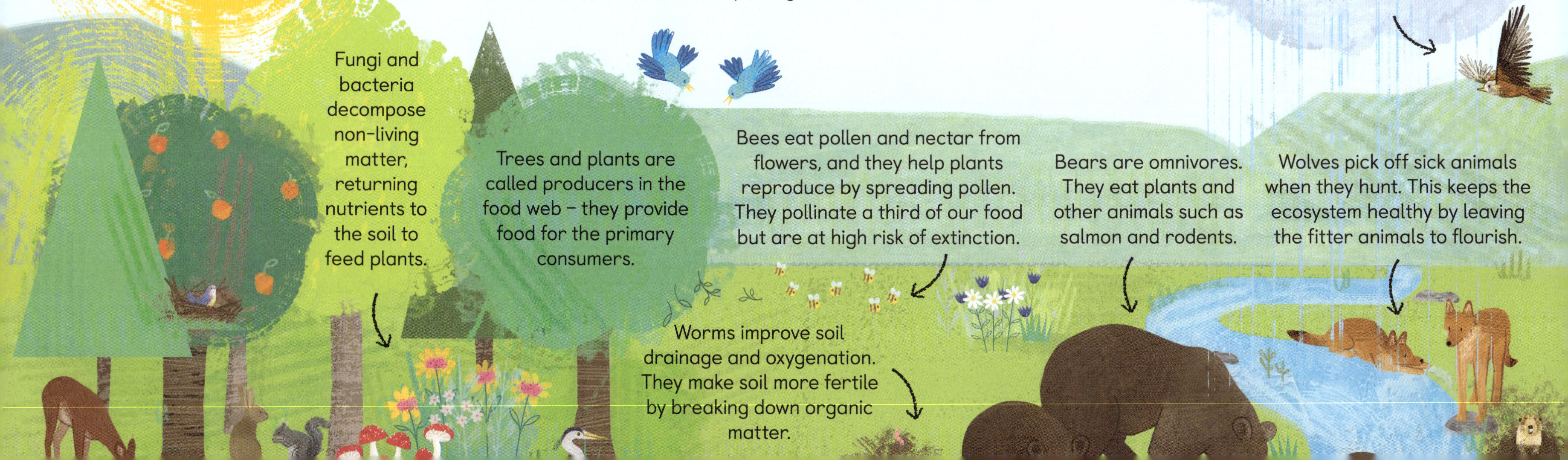

Bears are omnivores. They eat plants and other animals such as salmon and rodents.

Wolves pick off sick animals when they hunt. This keeps the ecosystem healthy by leaving the fitter animals to flourish.

After bears eat salmon, they poo in the forests, and their poo provides nitrogen for the trees.

Baleen whales are vital engineers of the ocean ecosystem! They eat deep in the ocean, then come to the surface to poo, providing fertilisers for the primary producers, such as algae, at the surface.

Coral reefs eat plankton and also get food from the algae that live inside them.

Kelp forests store carbon and are a vital source of food and shelter, but they are being wiped out by sea urchins, which take over when there aren't enough predators in the ecosystem.

Sea turtles are a primary consumer of sponges and seagrass and provide food for larger marine animals.

WHAT CAN WE DO?

Get involved in citizen science projects. Count species or record biodiversity in your area.

Feed birds and leave out water for them to drink and bathe in.

Grow bee-friendly flowers such as lavender or honeysuckle and avoid pesticides.

If you can, make a compost heap with all of your food scraps. They can become a hotbed of biodiversity!

changemaker

Sahithi Pingali, Bangalore, India

Sahithi was 15 when she began to wonder whether it could be the polluted waterways that were destroying the biodiversity of her local area. She was unable to find data to back up her theory, so she created WaterInsights, a kit and app allowing anyone to collect water samples and data.

WILDFIRES

Wildfires are uncontrolled blazes over land. They have been occurring naturally for millions of years, ignited by heat from the Sun or lightning strikes. Nowadays, around 90% of wildfires are caused by human carelessness, and climate change has been increasing their strength, number and length. This is because warmer temperatures make the land drier and more susceptible to fire. When plants and trees burn, they release large amounts of carbon dioxide, which contributes further to climate change.

DEADLY BLAZES

Australia's 2019/20 wildfires killed over one billion animals, 33 people and destroyed at least 180,000km² (69,498mi²) of land. During the fires, smoke blanketed 80% of the population.

LiDAR TECHNOLOGY

Smart technology such as LiDAR (light detection and ranging), which measures distances and maps 3D objects is being used to predict wildfires, alongside a growing network of cameras watching high risk areas.

changemaker

Anna Grace Hottinger
Minnesota, USA

Anna Grace was 15 when her sister was evacuated from a wildfire in California. This event encouraged her to protest against her government. She strikes every week and is involved with a climate group called Minnesota Can't Wait.

IN A GOOD LIGHT

Surprisingly, wildfires can sometimes be good for native vegetation because ashes are full of nutrients and feed the soil. In fact, some trees need the fires. Giant sequoia trees depend on the heat of the flames to split open their seeds, which allows them to grow. Wildfires can also clear weeds and non-native or diseased plants and insects.

Indigenous people have been managing off-season fires for a long time – burning leaves and old wood, and creating breaks in the forest, which prevent mega fires. Insects and animals can take shelter in the tree canopies. However, in ecosystems where wildfires are uncommon, they harm plant and animal life and damage infrastructure.

MIND THE GAP

Grazing animals or growing crops in the forest can slow down big fires by creating gaps in the trees and removing dead wood and leaves which can act as fuel for the fires.

DID YOU KNOW?

Wildfires are now happening as far north as the Arctic. 100 forest fires broke out in this region in June and July 2019 alone. The June fires in 2020 produced the same amount of CO_2 as Norway does in a year.

WHAT CAN WE DO?

Take great care around dry areas of land and forest and do not use anything with a flame. If you see a wildfire, report it immediately.

If you live in a wildfire zone, research the things that could reduce the spread of a fire, such as keeping your plants watered and removing dead plants and leaves.

Research indigenous knowledge about the natural world from your country and beyond. What can you find out that could be useful today?

A HOTTER WORLD

In 2019, global temperatures reached an average of 1.1°C (1.9°F) above pre-industrial levels. If we continue to create the same amounts of fossil fuel emissions, by around 2040 temperatures will rise by another 0.5°C (0.9°F). And by 2100 the increase could reach 4°C (7.2°F). Drastic emission cuts could help us stay within 1.5–2°C (2.7–3.6°F) of warming.

WHAT'S ALL THE FUSS ABOUT?

Half a degree may not sound like very much but the difference between a world that is 1.5°C (2.7°F) or 2°C (3.6°F) warmer will be life changing for humans, animals and ecosystems...

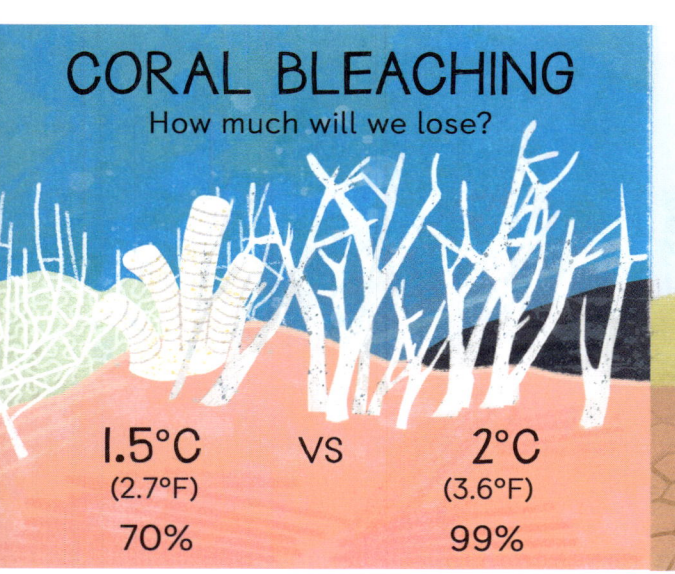

CORAL BLEACHING
How much will we lose?

1.5°C (2.7°F)	vs	2°C (3.6°F)
70%		99%

DROUGHT
How many people in cities will be affected by 2100?

1.5°C	vs	2°C
350 million people		410 million people

ECOSYSTEM LOSS
How much will we lose?

1.5°C	vs	2°C
7%		13%

SPECIES LOSS
How many plants and animals will we lose?

1.5°C	vs	2°C
6% insects		18% insects
8% plants		16% plants
4% vertebrates		8% vertebrates

RISE IN SEA LEVEL
How much of the global population will be impacted by 2100?

1.5°C	vs	2°C
46 million people 48cm (18.9in) sea level rise		49 million people 56cm (22in) sea level rise

EXTREME HEAT
How much of the global population will be exposed every five years?

1.5°C	vs	2°C
14%		37%

What do we need to do to stay within 1.5°C (2.7°F) of pre-industrial temperatures?

BY 2030 — Cut emissions by at least 50%

- Stop burning fossil fuels 
- Roll out renewable energy 
- Plant lots of trees and remove CO_2

BY 2050 — Emissions at net zero or below.

We do not know for certain that achieving net zero will stop our world from warming beyond 1.5°C (2.7°F).

Everyone will need to make changes – hopefully you will already be seeing changes when you read this. And as the young people featured in this book show, individuals can make a HUGE impact. What will you change?

Net zero means that the carbon emissions we produce are matched by activities that remove them from the atmosphere.

OUR PART

HOW WE'VE CONTRIBUTED TO THE CLIMATE CRISIS, AND IDEAS FOR MEANINGFUL CHANGE

OUR CARBON FOOTPRINT

A carbon footprint is the calculation of the total amount of all of the greenhouse gases produced by a given activity, person, country, business or product. Most activities produce carbon dioxide, even just breathing, so the idea of reducing your footprint might sound challenging at first!

THE SUM OF ALL PARTS

To understand the entire footprint of a product, we need to look at the emissions caused in every stage of its production and use. Let's look at the footprints of some everyday items.

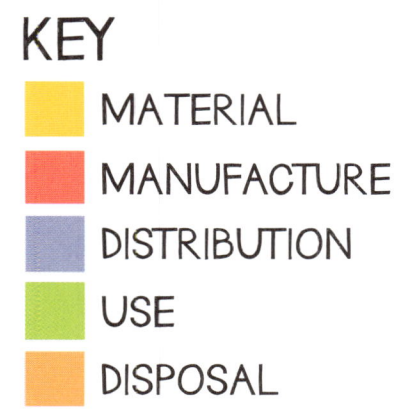

KEY

- **MATERIAL**
- **MANUFACTURE**
- **DISTRIBUTION**
- **USE**
- **DISPOSAL**

'CO_2e' is shorthand for carbon dioxide or equivalent greenhouse gases.

TOILET PAPER - 730G (25.5OZ) CO_2e
The biggest piece of this footprint is manufacturing (the processing and bleaching of the paper).

JEANS - 6KG (13.2LB) CO_2e
The manufacturing process and the use of the jeans (washed around 70 times in their lifetime) are the biggest factors. The material plays a part too, due to the fertiliser and energy used to grow and harvest the cotton.

SHAMPOO - 16.6KG (36.5LB) CO_2e
The greatest impact comes from our use of it, which is likely to be in a hot shower where a lot of energy is needed to heat the water.

SPORTS BAG - 35.3KG (77.8LB) CO_2e
Manufacturing is by far the biggest part of the footprint, as it will have involved spinning, weaving, dyeing and finishing.

changemaker

Azza Abdel Hamid Faiad
Alexandria, Egypt

When Azza was 16, she learnt that oil was not only damaging the environment but it was also very expensive for many people. She decided she needed to find a cheaper and sustainable alternative. So, after lots of research she discovered an inexpensive way to turn plastic waste, which Egypt has plenty of, into useful biofuel, and she won an award for her work.

WHAT'S YOUR FOOTPRINT?

There are lots of calculators out there but the good ones will ask you about the most important things that you do that produce greenhouse gases, such as what you eat, how you travel, what type of home you live in, how you heat it and the things you buy. Take a look at the World Wildlife Fund's calculator: **www.footprint.wwf.org.uk**. None of these calculators can take everything into consideration, but they are still useful.

FOOTPRINTS OF COUNTRIES AROUND THE WORLD

Today, China has the largest total carbon footprint of any country – accounting for more than one quarter of global CO_2. However, a large amount of China's footprint comes from making products for people around the world. China is followed by the USA (15%), the European Union (10%), India (7%) and Russia (5%).

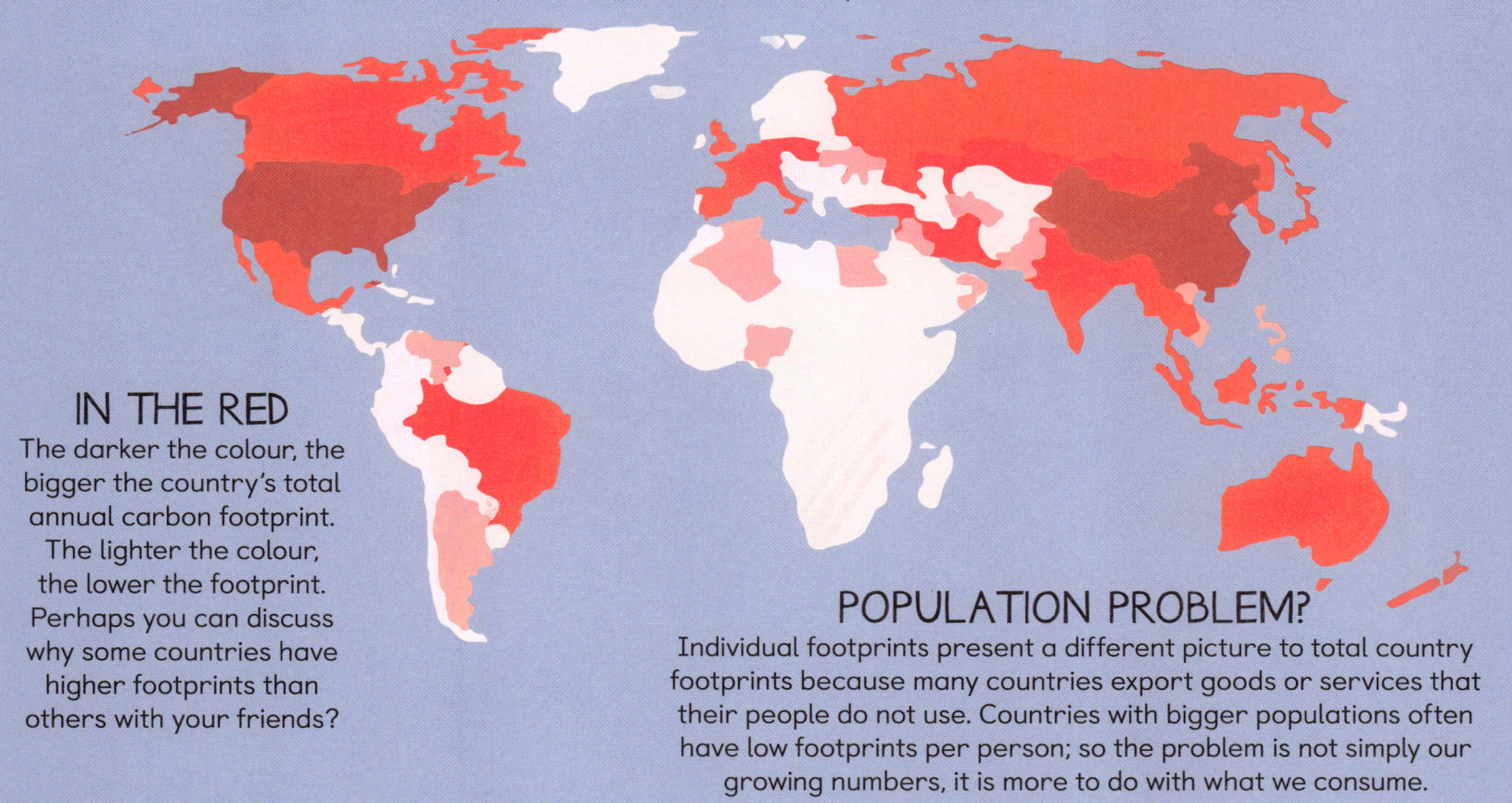

IN THE RED
The darker the colour, the bigger the country's total annual carbon footprint. The lighter the colour, the lower the footprint. Perhaps you can discuss why some countries have higher footprints than others with your friends?

POPULATION PROBLEM?
Individual footprints present a different picture to total country footprints because many countries export goods or services that their people do not use. Countries with bigger populations often have low footprints per person; so the problem is not simply our growing numbers, it is more to do with what we consume.

The global average carbon footprint per person per year is **4.7 tonnes** (5.2 short tons) CO_2.

North Americans and Canadians have the biggest average footprints - over **15 tonnes** (16.5 short tons) per person each year!

Sub-Saharan Africans have the smallest average footprints - around **0.1 tonnes** (0.1 short tons) per year for each person.

CLIMATE INJUSTICE
A UK resident will emit the same amount of CO_2 in five days as someone in Rwanda does in a whole year! Yet overall, climate change is affecting countries with smaller carbon footprints more severely than those countries with higher footprints.

WHAT CAN WE DO?

Cut down on flying. One long haul flight produces more carbon emissions than the average person in Burundi or Paraguay produces in a year.

Eat less meat and if you have pets, reduce or cut out their meat too. A vegan diet could reduce your carbon footprint by up to 20% but just cutting out beef will make a big difference too!

Heat and cool your home efficiently. You could save 320kg (705lb) of CO_2 a year by turning the thermostat for the heating down a degree.

Where possible, walk or cycle instead of getting in the car. Cutting out 8,050km (5,000mi) a year in the car will save more than a tonne of CO_2 – about 15% of the global average annual footprint.

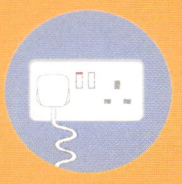

Try to switch off electrical appliances when not being used. You can save 30kg (66lb) of CO_2e every day by switching all of the power off at night in your house.

For a low-carbon snack, look no further than the banana! Grown in natural sunlight, transported by boat and without packaging, one banana produces about 80g (3oz) CO_2e.

Calculate your family's carbon footprint – and be honest!

41

OUR FOOD

The food we eat is responsible for about a quarter of the world's greenhouse gases every year, but different foods have wildly different 'foodprints'! Transportation, processing, storage and packaging all play a part, but the land used to produce the food is responsible for the biggest impact, not to mention those methane burps...

A MEATY PROBLEM

Meat has the largest footprint of all food, particularly when new land is cleared to raise livestock. The footprint of beef raised on land where forest has been converted into pasture is much higher than that for beef raised on existing pasture.

Chocolate also has a big footprint because trees are often cleared to grow the cacao beans it is made from. The footprint of farmed fish comes from the food it is fed, which can cause deforestation, and rice's footprint comes from the methane released from the paddy fields it is grown in.

CARBON FOODPRINTS

These figures show the average amount of greenhouse gases produced when 1kg (2.2lb) of that food is made, shown in kilograms of CO_2e.

BEEF 60KG (132LB)

CHEESE 21KG (46LB)

CHOCOLATE 19KG (42LB)

POULTRY 6KG (13LB)

FARMED FISH 5KG (11LB)

EGGS 4.5KG (10LB)

RICE 3.9KG (8.5LB)

MILK 3KG (6.6LB)

PEANUTS 2.5KG (5.5LB)

PEAS 1KG (2.2LB)

A TOMATO'S JOURNEY

Tomatoes can have a very small footprint if they are grown locally in the summer without pesticides and heating. But their impact can be almost as bad as beef if they are produced like this...

1. SEED PLANTED
First, seeds are planted in the soil in big heated tunnels made of plastic.

2. JUST ADD...
Water and fertiliser (made from fossil fuels).

3. PICK, PACK, PROCESS
Mechanically harvested and packed in plastic.

4. JOURNEY TO RETAILER
Planes or lorries used to transport.

5. IN THE SHOP
Stored in energy-hungry fridges under bright lights.

6. FROM SHOP TO HOME
Driven home in your car.

7. COOK & EAT
Grilled in a gas oven.

One kilogram (2.2lb) of organic cherry tomatoes grown in heated polytunnels creates 50kg (110lb) CO_2e.

Why not grow your own?

FOOD WASTE

30-40% of the food produced in the world is never eaten. That's a harsh reality in a world where an estimated 821 million people don't have enough to eat.

Buy ugly fruit and veg! Lots of produce is thrown away because its size, shape or colour isn't perfect.

Donate what you don't use to a food bank, community fridge or food waste app such as Olio.

Use every piece of the food you're cooking with – leave the skin on cucumbers and potatoes, and cook broccoli stems along with the florets as these often contain the most nutrients too.

DID YOU KNOW?

We could cut land used for farming by 75% (the size of the EU, USA, China and Australia all put together) if we stopped meat and dairy production!

Plan meals and use grocery lists or meal planning apps.

Make smoothies with over-ripe fruit, use wilting vegetables to make soups or just juice them all!

changemaker

Shalmali Tiwari
Raipur, India

Shalmali decided that leftovers from lunches shouldn't go to waste, so she set up a vermicomposting project at her school – the leftovers feed worms that produce compost. Shalmali used some of the compost on the school grounds and sold the rest to buy equipment for her school. She has been sharing her work and many other schools have taken on her ideas.

WHAT CAN WE DO?

Cut down on meat and eat more plants, such as fruit, veg, nuts, legumes and whole grains. Or why not try eating insects if you dare? High protein, low footprint. Grasshopper, anyone?

Reduce the amount of dairy you eat. Hemp milk has one of the lowest footprints of all alternative milks and it actually regenerates the soil as it grows!

Check your favourite chocolate bar to find out where the cacao came from and whether it contains palm oil. Look for the Rainforest Alliance logo to make sure it doesn't contribute to deforestation.

OUR CLOTHES

Before the 18th century, most people wove or knitted their own clothes out of wool. Things began to change with the Industrial Revolution in the 19th century. Machine-powered textile mills making large volumes of fabrics enabled clothes to be mass produced in factories. The invention of plastic in the early 20th century created a shift from natural cotton and wool to artificially made fabrics such as acrylic and polyester.

HARVESTING MATERIALS

SPINNING AND WEAVING

MACHINE OR HAND SEWING AND STITCHING

USE OF DYE

INDUSTRIAL WASHING

LABELLING

TRANSPORTATION

PACKAGING

SHOPS

MARKETING CAMPAIGNS

CLOTHES SOLD

WASHING AT HOME

LANDFILL

DIRTY FASHION

We are buying and then throwing away more clothes than ever before. The USA alone chucks out 9.3 million tonnes (10.2 million short tons) of clothes each year. Like our food, clothes go through a lot of stages before even being worn, and each stage uses a lot of energy. Sometimes, all of this happens only for clothes to be thrown away without even being worn!

Sadly, many of these clothes also have a large hidden cost. Often, very cheap clothes are made by factory workers who may be treated poorly, not paid enough to feed their families or forced to work in unsafe conditions. But it doesn't have to be this way. We can begin to think differently and love our clothes a little more!

DID YOU KNOW?
When we wash synthetic clothes, plastic fibres wash down the drain into the sea and are eaten by fish. One synthetic top alone can shed 1,900 microfibres.

DID YOU KNOW?
A rubbish truck full of clothes is taken to landfill every second, where they produce methane as they rot.

IT'S GETTING HOT IN HERE

Making clothes uses a lot of energy and produces a lot of greenhouse gases. Polyester has double the carbon footprint of cotton because it is made from oil, a fossil fuel.

Christmas jumpers have a big footprint because they are often made with acrylic, a plastic made from oil. This year, why not make your own or customise another jumper?

ARE YOUR CLOTHES TOXIC?

20% of global industrial water pollution comes from clothing factories. They release chemicals and dyes into water systems, causing huge damage to aquatic life. Cheap clothes sometimes contain substances that can be harmful to us too. Check the label and find out what you are putting against your skin.

THIRSTY WORK

Imagine all the water you've drunk over the last two and a half years. That is how much it takes to make one cotton T-shirt! Each year, 5 trillion litres (1.1 trillion gallons) of water is used for fabric dye to colour our clothes – enough to fill two million Olympic-sized swimming pools! This is far too much for our water-stressed world.

LOOKING GOOD

It is possible to create clothes in ways that are gentler on our people and planet…

Organically grown materials, such as hemp, are very helpful to the soil.

Fairtrade clothes are made by workers who are paid and treated fairly. Look for the FAIRTRADE Mark when you shop.

Some fabrics are biodegradable, such as Tencel, which is made from natural wood pulp.

If your passion is fashion, look into sustainable fabric development or textile design. Make beautiful clothes that don't cost the Earth!

changemaker

Maya Penn
Georgia, USA

Maya set up her own eco-fashion label (Maya's Ideas) when she was eight. She makes and sells sustainable accessories and clothes. She also makes and then donates reusable sanitary pads to girls without access to them. She gives 10% of her profits to charity and has even been on television… She's become a bit of a celebrity!

WHAT CAN WE DO?

- Buy second-hand clothes from charity shops or apps such as Depop.

- Be original and make your own clothes from the many free patterns available or customise them with accessories, embroidery and natural dyes.

- Ask a friend if you can borrow something for a special occasion or host a swishing (clothes swap) party.

- Turn down the washing machine's temperature, hang clothes out to dry and avoid power-hungry tumble dryers! Use a special laundry bag to catch plastic microfibres from synthetic clothes.

OUR HOMES

After transport and travel, our homes are generally the next biggest piece of our carbon footprint. And while we might not be able to change what our house is made of, there is a lot we can do to reduce the greenhouse gases that our house produces, as you'll see.

Solar panels can produce electricity and hot water. But if you can't fit them on your home, you could talk to your school about switching to solar. Visit www.solarforschools.co.uk for help.

Green roofs and living walls keep buildings cool in summer by absorbing the Sun's radiation and provide insulation in cooler months. They also combat air pollution by absorbing particles from the air.

Natural ventilation systems circulate air from outside to inside. They keep the air fresh and at a constant temperature.

Smart controls reduce energy usage in buildings by turning things on and off when they are needed or not in use.

Thick walls are excellent insulators.

Rainwater can be used to flush toilets to save water and energy.

Using wood as a building material turns the house into a carbon store, rather than a carbon emitter because CO_2 stays locked into the wood even once it is chopped down.

Batteries can store energy from solar panels that can be used when the Sun isn't shining. This energy could be used to charge an electric car!

Plants can improve indoor air quality.

Insulation, such as thick curtains, carpets and blinds is a very efficient way to reduce the need for heating and cooling.

Rainwater can be collected in water butts.

Triple glazing and smart glass control the amount of solar radiation a building absorbs.

Efficient LED lighting uses very little energy compared to older light bulbs.

Underfloor heating can be more efficient than radiators, and it keeps your feet lovely and warm!

District heating is a local heating source through insulated pipes, shared with neighbours.

Heat pumps take heat from either the air or the ground and transfer it efficiently to your home.

changemakers

Eco Squad, Hertfordshire, UK

The Eco Squad at Howe Dell Primary meet regularly to discuss how to make their Green Flag-awarded school even more eco-friendly. They use solar panels, collect rainwater for their veg patches and to flush their loos, and recycle or reuse everything they can. The squad also created an art exhibition from reused materials to engage the local community on environmental issues.

WHAT CAN WE DO?

Try taking a short shower instead of a bath to save water at home. But if you love having a bath, use the water on your garden or plants afterwards.

Do you need your room as warm or cool as it is? Could you change your clothes rather than turning on the heating or air conditioning?

Get rid of air leaks or your heating/cooling systems will have to work even harder! Drop a feather in front of doors, windows and chimneys and see if it is blown outwards. If it is, then plug those holes!

OUR STUFF

Almost every single thing around us has a carbon footprint and makes an impact on our world. From the chair you are sitting on, to a pen, to this book. If you added up the carbon footprint of everything in the room you are in now, you might be surprised at how big the number is...

THE HIDDEN CARBON COST

These figures are estimates of the footprints of some of the products (and people!) around us. They show the amount of greenhouse gases produced, handily transformed into kilograms of CO_2e, so we can compare them. They take into account what the products are made of, how they were produced and transported, and how we use and dispose of them.

A native broadleaf tree sucks up one tonne (1.1 short tons) of CO_2 in its lifetime.

Red rose
From garden 0kg
From heated greenhouse 2.1kg (4.6lb)

House (new two-bed)
80,000kg (176,370lb)

Apple
From garden 0g
From overseas 150g (5oz)

Paperback book
1kg (2.2lb)

500ml (17oz) plastic bottle of water
160g (5.6oz)

iPhone 11 (including use)
72kg (158lb)

Laptop (including use)
210kg (463lb)

Pair of jeans
6kg (13.2lb)

Toilet roll
Virgin paper 730g (25.8oz)
Recycled paper 450g (15.9oz)

Pair of shoes
11.5kg (25lb)

Baby (UK average over the course of a lifetime)
373,000kg (822,320lb)

Pint of tap water
0.14g (0.005oz)

Thick carpet
290kg (639lb)

48

WHAT A LOAD OF RUBBISH

What do you put in your rubbish bin that could be useful to someone or used for something else? Maybe that packaging could be used in a craft project? And that old toothbrush can be sent to a recycling programme (or used to clean your shoes!).

CIRCULAR ECONOMY

More companies are making their products using waste materials now, which is great news for the planet. Look out for skateboards made from old bottle tops, surfboards made out of old plastic bottles and wetsuits made from... old wetsuits!

SHOPPING CHALLENGE

Do you think you could live for a whole month without buying anything new, other than food? Why not give it a go with your family – you might be surprised at how much fun it is to salvage things, buy second-hand or borrow from friends.

PLASTIC PROBLEM

When plastic ends up in the ocean, most of it sinks to the deepest parts and is buried in sediment on the sea floor. Over time it breaks down into tiny microplastics and even smaller nanoplastics, which can get into the bloodstreams and cells of creatures, including us...

SAVE THE TURTLES

It is thought that more than half of all sea turtles have eaten plastic. A good reason to avoid single-use plastics wherever you can.

DID YOU KNOW?
The OceanHero search engine will clean one plastic bottle from the ocean for every five searches you carry out!

WHAT CAN WE DO?

Charity shops are great places to find new (to you!) books, clothes and toys. You can also donate anything you no longer want.

Have a look in your recycling bin to see if it contains single-use items that you could swap in future for reusable or waste-free alternatives.

Find out if there is a Library of Things close to you. You can rent almost anything from there at very low cost.

changemakers

Winners 1st prize — $10,000

Qier Qiu, Shanghai, China

Qier Qiu and her school friends realised how wasteful disposable chopsticks were and began chatting to people about the environmental benefits of reusable ones. They encouraged over 5,000 people to use reusable chopsticks and even developed a cleaning product for them! And in return they won a prize to help their school go green.

OUR TRAVEL

Travel can take us to see the most amazing places on Earth, but it can also have a big environmental footprint. The good news is that there are so many different options for how we can get around now, some with much lighter footprints than others. And remember, the journey is all part of the fun, so pack light (because this will also reduce your impact), get your seat by the window and enjoy.

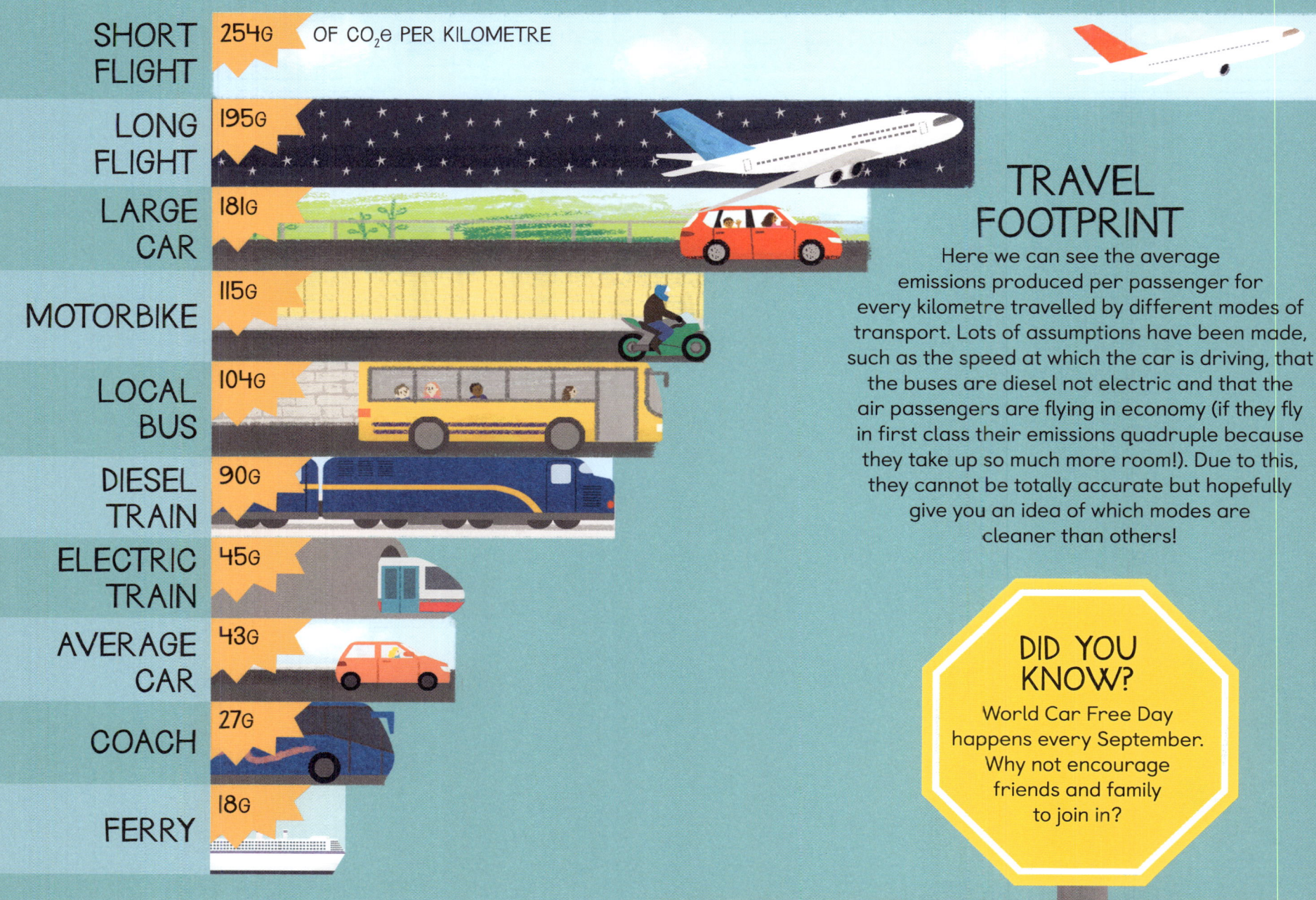

Mode	CO_2e per kilometre
SHORT FLIGHT	254g
LONG FLIGHT	195g
LARGE CAR	181g
MOTORBIKE	115g
LOCAL BUS	104g
DIESEL TRAIN	90g
ELECTRIC TRAIN	45g
AVERAGE CAR	43g
COACH	27g
FERRY	18g

TRAVEL FOOTPRINT

Here we can see the average emissions produced per passenger for every kilometre travelled by different modes of transport. Lots of assumptions have been made, such as the speed at which the car is driving, that the buses are diesel not electric and that the air passengers are flying in economy (if they fly in first class their emissions quadruple because they take up so much more room!). Due to this, they cannot be totally accurate but hopefully give you an idea of which modes are cleaner than others!

DID YOU KNOW?
World Car Free Day happens every September. Why not encourage friends and family to join in?

WHAT CAN WE DO?

Try slow travel on your next holiday. Take the train instead of flying and the bus instead of a taxi, if you can. If you really want to get to know somewhere, stay with locals.

Use public transport, walk or cycle wherever you can. Some cities offer free public transport now to help keep air pollution down. Cycling is the most efficient form of transport. With the same amount of energy, you travel three times faster by bike than by foot! You could hire an electric bike for a longer journey.

If you are planning a trip and want to find out the most carbon efficient way to get there, take a look at www.ecopassenger.org

INSPIRATION

LET'S MEET SOME MORE AMAZING YOUNG PEOPLE AND TALK ABOUT YOUR FUTURE...

GROUNDBREAKERS

Greta Thunberg, Sweden

In August 2018, 16-year-old Greta started protesting outside parliament in Stockholm with a sign saying, "School strike for climate". People started to join her, and by March 2019, 1.6 million children had gone on strike around the world, demanding action. In September 2019, Greta inspired more than four million people to take part in a global climate strike.

"There is hope – I've seen it – but it does not come from the governments or corporations, it comes from the people."

Ayakha Melithafa, South Africa

Ayakha is a spokesperson for the African Climate Alliance and has called for an immediate suspension on the extraction of coal, oil and gas in South Africa.

"People who are older aren't paying as much attention because they will not be as affected. They don't take us seriously, but we want to show them we are serious."

Jaden Anthony, USA

When he was just nine, Jaden wrote *Kid Brooklyn*, a graphic novel series that strives to introduce children to environmental and social issues.

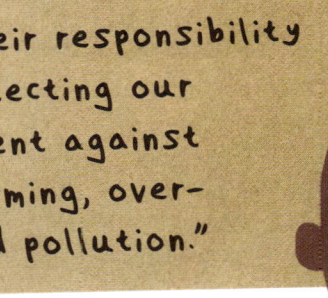

"I want to teach kids about their responsibility for protecting our environment against global warming, over-fishing and pollution."

Xiuhtezcatl Martinez, USA

Xiuhtezcatl has been a climate activist since he was six. He is the youth director of worldwide conservation organisation Earth Guardians and he makes hip-hop music about climate change.

"The future of our generation is at stake."

Mone Fousseny, Mali

Mone has been part of the Citizens' Boycott – raising awareness about how boycotting certain multinational products can be helpful to the environment.

"I want to tell the people of planet Earth […] that we are all […] responsible for global warming. There is still time to act locally, in our homes, our villages, our cities."

Oscar Alateras, Australia

Oscar had decided that he would study climate change further and then do something about it after university. But at the beginning of 2018, he realised that he didn't need to wait. He has now written a book – *The Truth About Our World*.

"We are never too young to change our world for the better."

Brianna Fruean, Samoa

Aged 11, Brianna became a founding member of the environmental group 350 Samoa – the organisation's youngest country co-ordinator.

"The young people of the Pacific are now experiencing what young people around the world will experience tomorrow. [...] Our slogan is: 'We're not drowning. We're fighting.'"

Zach Haynes, UK

When Zach was ten, he started a hugely popular environmental blog. He has written articles, given interviews and talks, and contributed to workshops about how nature organisations can better engage young people. Zach is also a young ambassador for the #iwill4nature campaign.

"I have found support on social media and learnt that by joining up with others we can make a big difference."

Marinel Sumook Ubaldo, Philippines

Marinel lost her house and all her belongings after super typhoon Haiyan hit the Philippines. She then testified in court against some of the world's biggest energy companies, attempting to prove their part in climate change.

"I want world leaders to commit to minimising greenhouse gases. I want them to help vulnerable countries adapt to the unavoidable effects of climate change."

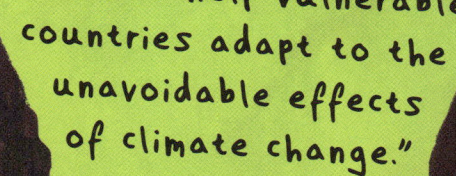

Nadia Nazar & Jamie Margolin, USA

These friends were 16 when they co-founded Zero Hour – a youth-led climate organisation – with two other friends. They organise strikes, marches, lobbies and festivals, and also raise money.

"We must speak out because it is our lives that are on the line. I am especially proud of building a movement that is run by women of colour."

HOW TO GET ACTIVE

Everyone has their own reason for wanting to make change or get involved in the climate movement. Maybe it's your love of animals and the natural world? Or maybe you care about how people are being affected by this crisis? Discover your passion and let it motivate you!

Daniela Torres Perez
Dani is co-founder of UK Student Climate Network, a group of young people taking to the streets to protest the government's lack of action on the climate crisis. They organised over 850 demonstrations in 2019.

DANI'S TOP TIPS

1: SPREAD THE WORD
Share information about the ecological crisis. Use social media if you have it – you could set up a Facebook page; print posters and leaflets; reach out to community groups, schools and other environmental organisations; get in touch with your local press to get coverage and talk to everyone you know about the climate crisis!

2: START AN ECO SQUAD
Get a group of friends together to discuss some of the important climate challenges in your area and what you could do to help. It might be a campaign to inform and engage people, a fundraising event or a clothes swap. Think of ways to reduce your carbon footprint and how to make your school or home more eco-friendly.

3: STAYING SAFE AT A MARCH
Climate marches are safe spaces, but you must go with a responsible adult. Marching can be tiring, so bring snacks and water! Don't forget to get creative and bring placards. They spread the message and are super fun to make! There are always chants and songs during marches that are easy to learn and great to join in with.

4: FIND YOUR NEAREST STRIKE
Check the Fridays for Future website – www.fridaysforfuture.org or www.ukscn.org if you're in the UK. If you can't find a strike near you then create your own! You'll need permission from your parent or guardian to miss school, and don't forget that you'll need to be accompanied by a responsible adult when on strike.

5: GET INVOLVED!

• UKSCN are running a campaign for schools to declare climate emergencies #Classrooms4Climate. Why not get your school involved?

• Check out #TalksForFuture – a live, weekly webinar from Fridays for Future hosting scientists, journalists and activists. Look up #ClimateStrikeOnline too. Join the online fight against climate change and learn whilst you do it!

• The World Wildlife Fund has great online resources: www.wwf.org.uk/get-involved/schools/resources

CLIMATE CHANGER

Eytan Yoles Stanton, Activist from New York

Eytan is an artist, environmental activist and gardener. He researched the most effective ways his school could reduce its carbon footprint, which helped win a sustainable infrastructure grant for the school. During his gap year, he studied organic agriculture and permaculture design and is planning to study environmental design at university.

WHAT GOT YOU PERSONALLY INVOLVED IN THE CLIMATE MOVEMENT?

At age ten, I started to appreciate not only eating, but cooking. So, I began to garden. Nature, I soon learnt, was in peril because of us. Since then I have grown more passionate about learning, exploring and changing the ways that humans live their lives to limit our damage to the Earth. This appreciation, respect and awe towards nature has continued to inspire me.

WHAT ARE THE MOST EFFECTIVE WAYS TO ENGAGE, EMPOWER AND ACTIVATE OTHER PEOPLE ON CLIMATE CHANGE?

Identify the ways of engaging with issues that speak the most to you. I often do research, read and write articles, and share the scientific background of the climate crisis. Teaching about gardening is another way I activate others to care more for nature. Share climate issues in the way that makes you most passionate, whether it be through articles, painting, food or any other form of expression.

WHAT DO YOU SUGGEST FOR THOSE WHO DON'T WANT TO STRIKE OR MARCH?

Striking is the tip of the iceberg of things that you can do to take action. Taking action from home literally starts with your home. Share the importance of reducing carbon emissions with your family and explain that it doesn't have to radically alter their lives. Small changes can have big benefits.

AND FOR THOSE WHO AREN'T ON SOCIAL MEDIA?

Social media can be an effective way to spread information but is by no means the only way to engage. Making sustainable choices goes a long way. It sends a message to the world and to those who see your choices. Sharing your ideas with family, friends or teachers is an incredible way to spread awareness without the use of social media. There are also local organisations, groups and networks to get involved with that have events and actions.

HOW DO YOU PREVENT YOURSELF FROM FEELING OVERWHELMED BY THIS ISSUE?

Environmental issues and the global failure to address them is scary, frustrating and exhausting. I find great comfort in nature itself. Every time the rain falls, a plant grows in the cracks of a pavement or a bird sings, recognise the amazingness of it. We are part of something much larger than our communities, humanity or Earth. We are part of the wonderful story of life in our universe, and that is a privilege that keeps me at peace.

WHAT'S YOUR ADVICE FOR OTHERS LIKE YOU WHO MIGHT BE INTERESTED IN PERMACULTURE?

I encourage visiting a local permaculture institution, whether it be a school or nearby garden. When the time comes, I highly recommend the Permaculture Design Course and getting some hands-on experience.

GREEN FUTURES

Do you want to get paid to save the world? Take a look at some of these exciting careers that can contribute to a thriving planet, and find out which higher education courses and subjects you could study or get experience in.

RENEWABLE ENERGY SPECIALIST

Are you amazed by the heat of the Sun? Or the strength of the wind and the waves? They will soon provide most of our power, but we need people like you to work out how to use and maintain them and make them as efficient and clean as possible. Study engineering, materials science, marine science, marine engineering, marine technology, electronics or manufacturing.

HYDROLOGIST

Water is soon going to be our most in-demand resource. As a hydrologist you could work all over the world, looking into local or national water issues, from flood controls to groundwater contamination. Study hydrology, geoscience, environmental science, or engineering.

ECO-HOUSE BUILDER OR DESIGNER

Do you love architecture? Would you like to create buildings that are zero energy and waste? Or homes that have a positive impact on our planet?

Study engineering, construction, property development or architecture.

REWILDING SPECIALIST

We can all look after the land, but this can be a full time job too. If you feel passionate about the natural world, then study and read about rewilding and regeneration. You could find yourself in some of the most incredible places on Earth.

ENVIRONMENTAL ARTIST

We need writers, actors, poets, photographers, musicians and artists to get people engaged with the climate crisis. Your route to this career could be through art, media, journalism, film, music or marketing qualifications, but you can start producing your own material any time!

CLIMATE OR NATURAL SCIENTIST

Study any of the sciences that interest you, and help us to better understand our world so that we can protect and enjoy it. We have only voyaged into about 5% of the oceans, and there are millions of species still to be discovered. You might even get something named after you!

FARMER OR AGRONOMIST

We need to get really creative in order to produce more food with less land and make innovative biofuels with waste materials. Maybe that is where you come in? From hydroponics to hemp, there is so much scope here for problem solvers. Study agronomy, agriculture, food science, bioengineering, microbiology, biochemistry or biophysics.

SOIL SCIENTIST

We cannot live without healthy soil, so we need more people to understand how to bring it back to life and make it more resistant to our changing climate. Anyone who knows about soil will be in demand! Study soil sciences, permaculture or microbiology.

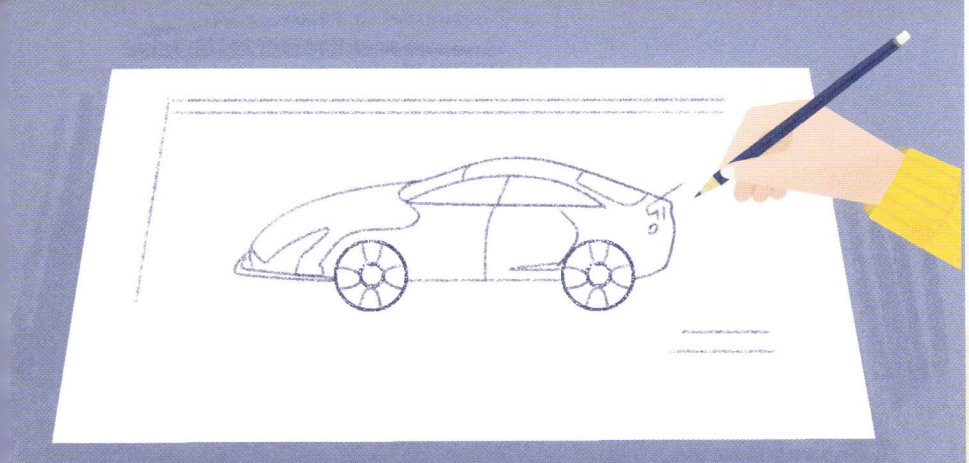

ENVIRONMENTAL LAWYER OR POLITICIAN

If you like the idea of standing up for our planet or for people who are being unfairly treated, then politics or law could be the right career for you. Study politics or environmental law, and read the news every day to see how these professions can make positive change.

GREEN TRANSPORT ENGINEER OR DESIGNER

Want to help build or design the world's greenest, cleanest and fastest modes of transport? Then study engineering, electronics, design or mechanics. If you want to race electric cars, go-karting is a great place to start!

GREEN PRODUCT DESIGNER

Do you want to design new products that could provide solutions to the climate crisis? Products that make it easy for people to save water, reduce waste or cut their carbon footprint? Study technology, product design or engineering and read about the latest planet-saving developments. Jot down your ideas and share them with your parents or a teacher. Could you build a prototype?

AIR QUALITY SPECIALIST

We all need to breathe clean air, and we will be monitoring it much more closely in years to come. If this appeals to you, then study environmental science or engineering.

WHAT NEXT?

How do you feel now, having read this book alongside
any other information about the climate crisis?

INSPIRED   ANGRY   FRUSTRATED   HAPPY
OVERWHELMED   POWERFUL   OPTIMISTIC
   INTERESTED
POWERLESS   ANNOYED   WORRIED   PESSIMISTIC
DETERMINED   SCARED   ENERGISED
SAD   EXCITED   TIRED

Maybe you feel all of these things, maybe none of them. We each respond to things differently because we are all unique. However you feel, it's good to talk about it! So why don't you speak to your family or friends, and see how they feel about things? Hopefully this book has shown you that there is still so much to feel optimistic about...

There are so many amazing young (and older) people around the world
who care and who are making enormous, positive changes.

We know exactly what needs to be done to support our planet.

We have huge amounts of knowledge about how to live sustainably,
especially amongst indigenous peoples.

We can make big changes quickly when we want to. This has been proved
by the global reaction to the coronavirus (COVID-19) outbreak.

We know that nature bounces back very quickly if we let it.
Those in power are beginning to listen to the voices of the people,
but we still need more people to stand up for the planet.

Perhaps reading this book has made you want to take action and add your voice. Do you feel like trying out some of our suggestions? Could you get friends involved? Maybe you are inspired by the actions of the amazing changemakers? Take it easy, though. Don't try to do too much at once!

Do you want to learn more? There is a lot of information out there. **WWF.org** is a good place to start. And look out for inspiration from indigenous practices too. Many indigenous cultures understand and work in harmony with nature.

Do you want to get involved with the climate movement? Perhaps by speaking at your school assembly, to your family or just with a friend? You might prefer to write to your local politician to ask them what they plan to do. You could even give them some ideas!

Are you creative? Maybe you would like to write or draw about climate change? Or would you rather sing or create something to express how you feel about it? There are lots of artistic communities around the world who use art to express themselves and engage with meaningful topics. They would welcome your contribution.

Perhaps you would like to connect more with nature? You could do some gardening or explore the great outdoors with your family. Take time out to listen to and observe wildlife, and try taking off your shoes... reconnecting with the soil can be life-changing in itself.

If, on the other hand, you don't feel like taking action right now, then that is fine too. Simply having an understanding of the issue and just thinking and talking about it is very powerful. Our planet needs us, and we need our planet. Let's all be the change we want to see.

> "Every single person on this Earth has the power to change the world."
> — Shalvi Shakshi, from Fiji, addressing world leaders when she was ten years old.

GLOSSARY

Agriculture – Farming, including growing and harvesting food and raising animals.

Agroforestry – A method of farming that involves growing trees and crops in the same area.

Agronomy – The science of farming, including the study of soil, crops and animals, and how to improve food production.

Albedo effect – The effect whereby light surfaces reflect more heat than dark surfaces. Global warming causes ice to melt, meaning that areas of the Earth's surface become less reflective. This causes the Earth to heat up further and more ice to melt.

Alga (plural is algae) – A plantlike organism that lives in or near water, which doesn't have leaves, roots or stems, such as seaweed or pond scum.

Algorithm – A list of rules to follow in order to solve a problem.

Ammonia – A gas used in fertilisers and cleaning liquids, as well as for purifying water and keeping things cold.

Aquifer – An underground area of rock containing groundwater that has seeped through the soil.

Atmosphere – The gases that surround a planet.

Atom – Tiny particles, which are the building blocks of all matter.

Aviation – Activities related to flying aircraft.

Biochar – Charcoal that can be made from waste materials such as rice husks.

Biodiversity – The range and number of different plant and animal species. If a place is biodiverse, it has a great number and variety of living creatures.

Biodynamic farming – A form of organic farming that treats the farm as its own ecosystem and encourages biodiversity.

Biofuel – A fuel made from the remains of living things or their waste.

Biomass – Living matter or its waste that can be used as a fuel (biofuel is made from biomass).

CO_2 – The chemical formula for carbon dioxide: carbon (C) and oxygen (O). It is a greenhouse gas found in our atmosphere.

CO_2e (carbon dioxide equivalent) – A unit of measure for carbon footprints, which shows that various greenhouse gases have been converted into the equivalent amount of carbon dioxide with the same global warming potential.

Carbon dioxide storage – Keeping carbon dioxide out of the atmosphere by holding it in other matter, such as underground rocks or plants.

Carbon footprint – The amount of carbon dioxide released into the atmosphere as the result of the activities of an individual or organisation.

Carbon sink – A natural area that absorbs more carbon dioxide than it releases.

Circular economy – A model of production and consumption that aims to extend the life cycle of products and minimise waste.

Citizen science – Scientific work, such as data collection, that is carried out by people without qualifications in order to help scientists.

Climate change – A long-term change in weather and temperature across the world or a part of the world.

Combustion – The process of burning.

Conservation – The act of protecting and preserving something, such as an area of land or species of wildlife.

Deforestation – The act of cutting down trees across a large area in order to use the land for another purpose.

Drone – An aircraft without a pilot, which is controlled by someone on the ground.

Drought – Dry weather and a shortage of water over a long period.

Ecosystem – Made up of all the living and non-living things found in an area, along with the ways they relate to and depend on each other.

Emission – The release of something, such as smoke or fumes.

Erosion – The action of something being worn away over time, usually by a natural force such as water.

Feedback loop – A chain of actions where the final outcome causes the first process to start again.

Fertiliser – A substance added to soil to help plants grow.

Floodplain – A flat area of land around a river that is prone to flooding.

Fluorinated gas – Gas that has had fluorine added to it. Fluorinated gases are used in industry but are damaging to the environment because they are greenhouse gases.

Food chain – The movement of energy caused when one organism eats another, which is then eaten by another, which in turn is eaten by another.

Fossil fuel – Fossil fuels are made from animal and plant remains that have changed under pressure over millions of years into new substances, such as oil, coal or gas. They release carbon dioxide when burnt, so contribute to global warming.

Fugitive emissions – Gases that are released by accident, such as in pipe leaks, often in an industrial setting.

Fungus (plural is fungi) – An organism, such as a mushroom or yeast, which is similar to a plant but doesn't have stems, roots or leaves. It usually feeds off decaying material.

Generator – A machine that turns movement energy into electricity.

Geological – Related to the substances that make up the Earth's surface and the layers beneath.

Geothermal – Associated with the heat inside the Earth.

Glacier – A large volume of ice that moves slowly over a long period of time.

Global warming – The long-term temperature increase happening around the world caused by the heat-trapping effect of greenhouse gases such as carbon dioxide.

Greenhouse effect – A process that occurs in our atmosphere in which gases trap the Sun's heat around the Earth, just as the glass of a greenhouse keeps heat inside.

Greenhouse gas – A gas that stops the Sun's heat reflecting away from the Earth and traps it in our atmosphere.

Green hydrogen – Hydrogen produced when an electrical current, generated using renewable energy, is passed through water to separate the hydrogen gas from the oxygen.

Green wall – A large belt of trees planted to combat climate change.

H_2O – The chemical formula for water – used because this liquid is composed of hydrogen (H) and oxygen (O).

Hemp – A group of plants with a lot of fibre, which can be used for making strong textiles, such as rope.

Hydroelectric – Related to the creation of electricity from the movement of water.

Hyperloop – A transport system made up of huge tubes in which magnetic force moves the vehicles.

Ice cap – A glacier that is less than 50,000km^2 (19,000mi^2).

Ice sheet – A vast area of ice covering more than 50,000km^2 (19,000 mi^2).

Indigenous – Originating or naturally occurring somewhere. Often used to describe people.

Infrastructure – The systems and facilities that enable society to function. Examples include roads and power supplies.

Insulator – A material that does not let heat pass through it easily.

Kinetic – Related to movement.

LED (Light Emitting Diode) – A type of light source that is long-lasting compared to many other light bulbs.

LiDAR – Stands for Light Detection and Ranging. Light is sent out and reflected off objects. The time it takes for the light to return helps scientists work out where these objects are, along with the direction in which the air that the light is travelling through is moving. This can be used to discover how wildfires will spread.

Livestock – Farm animals.

Marine heatwave – A prolonged period of high temperatures in an area of the ocean.

Meteorology – The study of the Earth's atmosphere, including weather and climate.

Methane – A greenhouse gas produced by wetlands, livestock and landfill sites.

Methanol – A chemical that can be used as clean-burning fuel.

Mineral – Solid substances that can be found underground, such as coal.

Monoculture – An area of farmland on which one crop is grown, or just one kind of animal is kept.

Natural hazard – An event that can cause loss of life and extreme damage. Examples include flooding and droughts.

Non-renewable (energy) – A limited amount exists that cannot be replaced once it has been used.

Nuclear energy – Created when atoms are split apart or fused together. It is a type of renewable energy.

Organic farming – Food grown without chemical pesticides or fertilisers, and livestock reared without antibiotics.

Organism – A living animal or plant.

Oscillate – To move back and forth.

Ozone layer – A layer of Earth's atmosphere that protects living things from the harmful radiation of the Sun.

Permaculture – A system of growing crops and plants in such a way that they can sustain themselves over a long period of time, echoing natural systems.

Pesticide – A chemical used to kill unwanted insects, rodents or weeds.

Photosynthesis – The process through which plants convert light energy into food.

Pliocene era – A period of time spanning the interval from 5.3 million to 2.6 million years ago.

Power grid – A network of cables used to distribute electricity over an area.

Primary consumer – In the food chain, an animal that eats primary producers.

Primary producer – In the food chain, a plant that makes food from the Sun and is then eaten by an animal.

Radiation – The energy given out by something. For example, heat or light.

Radioactive – Having or creating (often harmful) energy from the breaking up of atoms.

Rehabilitation – Restoring something that has been damaged to a good condition.

Renewable (energy) – Resources that are not reduced by use, such as the wind, tide and the Sun.

Resource – A source or supply of something useful.

Rewild – Returning an area to its natural state, including reintroducing plants and animals.

Sea ice – Frozen seawater that floats on the sea's surface.

Sea level – The level of the sea where it meets the land.

Silicon – An element found in rocks and sand, used for making electronic machines.

Soil degradation – A decline in the quality of the soil.

Storm wave – A large wave of water produced by high winds and stormy conditions.

Synthetic – Made from artificial materials.

Tsunami – A huge sea wave, usually caused by an earthquake.

Turbine – A machine in which a liquid or gas causes a wheel or blades to turn.

Unrefined – Used to describe something that hasn't gone through any chemical processes and is in its natural state.

Vermicomposting – The use of earthworms to turn organic waste into compost.

Vertical farming – A kind of farming that involves growing plants in vertical layers. Instead of soil, the crops are fed using water vapour and a nutrient solution.

Warming stripes – Pictures of stripes that are used to represent the increase in temperature over time. Blues are used for cooler temperatures and reds for warmer ones.

ABOUT THE CREATORS

GEORGINA STEVENS - THE AUTHOR

Georgina is a sustainability advisor, writer and campaigner. She advises organisations and individuals on how they can have a positive impact on our planet. She also organises Be The Change events to help people step into their power and understand how we can all effect major change, even through small actions. And when she's not writing, you can find her forest bathing or planting things. www.georginastevens.org

I wanted to show my son Rafael how powerful we all are in making positive change, so I wrote him a funny story about a shark and plastic pollution, and that is how I started writing children's books. I also really wanted to showcase how many amazing people there are around the world already doing incredible work to safeguard our wonderful planet. And that is where the idea for Climate Action came from. The hardest part, while doing research for the book, was choosing which young people to include because there are so many of them — all so unique and impressive! I cannot thank them enough for their efforts and energy.

KATIE REWSE - THE ILLUSTRATOR

Katie is an illustrator based in Bournemouth, on the South coast of England, where she studied for both her BA and MA in illustration. Katie is particularly interested in how illustration can be used to inspire positive change and she finds inspiration in the outdoors, travel and adventure. www.katierewse.com

Looking after our home, planet Earth, is really important to me. As an outdoor adventurer and nature enthusiast, protecting the things that I love seems only natural. The more I have learnt about climate change though, the more I am challenged by the bigger picture and the concerns for how future humanity will be affected. We are incredibly lucky to live on Earth, and it is only fair that future generations should be able to enjoy this home too.

TREE PLANTING PROJECT

A tree will be planted for every copy of this edition sold in the UK, through the TreeSisters charity. Their mission is to restore the Earth through tropical reforestation and they are working towards a goal of planting a billion trees a year. So far, TreeSisters have planted many millions of trees across Kenya, Madagascar, Brazil, Cameroon, Nepal, West Papua, Mozambique and India. Part of their work is with women; they offer educational tools, resources, courses and community with the aim to empower and inspire women to take leadership roles in environmental protection and restoration. www.treesisters.org